Bad Mind

Karen Cavalli

Aster Press
An imprint of Blue Fortune Enterprises, LLC

BAD MIND
Copyright © 2019 by Karen Cavalli.

All rights reserved. Printed in the United States of America. No part of this book may be used or reproduced in any manner whatsoever without written permission except in the case of brief quotations embodied in critical articles or reviews.

This book is a work of fiction. Names, characters, businesses, organizations, places, events and incidents either are the product of the author's imagination or are used fictitiously. Any resemblance to actual persons, living or dead, events, or locales is entirely coincidental.

For information contact :
Blue Fortune Enterprises, LLC
Aster Press
P.O. Box 554
Yorktown, VA 23690
http://blue-fortune.com

Cover design by Wesley Miller, WAMCreate, wamcreate.co

ISBN: 978-1-948979-23-8

First Edition: October 2019

Dedication

To Barbara Anderson, who inspired me; to the many individuals around the world who shared their experiences with me and taught me about the incredible kindness of this particular community; and, as always, to my husband Tom, for all things.

Praise for *Bad Mind*:

Karen Cavalli writes movingly and well about her life, which has been enriched throughout by otherworldly experiences. She describes her interactions with the people, in the flesh and in the spirit, who have touched her life and who have been touched, in turn, by hers. Some of her experiences are "encounters with aliens." All of her life has been filled with emotionally and spiritually rich events that illuminate the strength and survival of her own spirit as well as the strength of the human spirit.

Don C. Donderi, PhD
Associate Professor (retired)
McGill University, Montreal

Table of Contents

Preface i
Why Can't We Think About Aliens? 7
ET in the Gulf 11
Just Another Face of Spirit 27
My Journey Through Stupid Times 31
Bad Mind 39
An Old-Fashioned Fairy 53
I Dream of Djinni 57
The Goddess of Sloth 63
Midwestern Medium 67
Layers 73
A Visit to Usha's 85

Preface

BAD MIND **IS A COLLECTION** of essays that examines and muses about the state of spirit in America through the telling of individuals' real-life encounters with otherworldly beings. Several of these essays have been published in traditional and online publications. I gathered these stories after I came out as an experiencer of anomalous encounters and inadvertently discovered there are many, many average folks such as myself with similar encounters. However, these people felt they couldn't talk about these experiences, mostly from fear of ridicule and possible job loss. Through observation, interviews, telling the gathered stories, weaving in my own encounters and related musings and referencing history, I explore this western taboo and what it says about our American state of spirit.

Taboo is a strong word; however, the definition fits: prohibited, restricted or frowned upon by social custom. Robert Irwin captures the spirit of the term in his work, *Memoirs of a Dervish: Sufis, Mystics and the Sixties* when he writes, "Like body odours, ecstasy is something that nice people don't talk about." If you talk about body odor in general conversation, the listeners are likely to change how they view you; the same is true if you speak of your individual encounter with something other-worldly. As Narielle Living put it, talking about your one-on-one experience with an anomalous being "kind of puts you in the same position as being a Jewish girl at Sunday Catholic mass. Nobody will kick you out of the building but they sure do look at you funny."

The tone of the essays is sincere though the voice is often irreverent, a nod to my outer, smarty-pants self that developed as a cover in my twenties. Back then, even those of us who were intelligent, educated and open-minded shut the intellectual doors on the topic of the "paranormal." I was living near Virginia Beach, Virginia, home of Edgar Cayce's Association for Research and Enlightenment, but it was an oddity few in my circle spoke about. Best to lead with a derisive tone, I discovered, when speaking about dubious topics; such a tone provided armor should anyone hoot, and the guise was easily shrugged off if it met with sincere interest. During those years, for me it never did. The first time I encountered the balm of sincere interest was when I was nearing the age of fifty.

When I came out as an experiencer in 2014, I met multitudes of sweet people who had stories to tell about their personal experiences with beings our American culture would have us believe are imaginary: fairies, ghosts, demons, men in black, extraterrestrials, extradimensiononals, loved ones passing from this world into the next. I was moved by their sincerity and their heartfelt response to encounters with the anomalous. They seemed happy to be able to speak to someone who had had similar experiences. Most of them feared speaking openly about these experiences because of imagined consequences: they would be ridiculed; they would lose their jobs, their careers and any chance at ever making a decent living; their friends and family would desert them.

I lived with that fear for many years. I too shut out the inhabitants of other worlds who visited me.

How did it come to be that we have the power and luxury to shut out inhabitants of the spirit world? Was this particularly American? Do Americans not play well with the inhabitants of the murky spirit world and so we must keep them at arm's length? Just how prevalent is the experience of encountering anomalous beings in the US? What can we learn from those cultures with more experience with the inhabitants of the spirit world?

I embarked on a journey to find out. I began asking nearly everyone I met if they'd ever had an experience with the paranormal. Everyone was eager to help me spread the word; all gave me permission to use their stories in my writing, though some requested anonymity.

A picture of this planet's terrestrial citizens began to emerge. Many of us live a very different reality from that which our culture leaders would have us believe is the acceptable, right way to live and believe. I'm reminded of something a friend said to me in about 2005 when I was in Tianjin, China, on business. He said Chinese citizens quietly do and believe what they want despite what their country's leaders say they should do and believe.

We in the U.S. are on the forefront of technological advances but our American spirit life has not kept pace. We hold our devices close but keep the spirit world inhabitants at arm's length, engaging in stalking and hunting them as though they are prey while at the same time publicly professing skepticism they exist.

I offer a new perspective on this phenomenon. I present untold stories of average folk like myself and allow the reader to come to their own conclusions. A delving into history reveals a time when imaginal and rational realms were joined. Anomalous beings or extreme other had a place in our culture. We recognized these entities as inhabitants of the spirit world. Even though our American forebears shut them out a little over 200 years ago, that hasn't stopped these extraordinary entities from continuing to manifest in our average, everyday lives.

Like some of those anomalous beings who have presented themselves to everyday humans, spirit cannot be seen but can be felt. How your average American comes to terms with these encounters reveals lives of spirit required by taboo to remain hidden and silent.

I believe our inability to think about anomalous beings intelligently holds us back from collectively integrating something key about our world. We can find aid in the writings of contemporary people of science, for example, physicist Tom Campbell and cellular biologist Bruce Lipton, who can demonstrate how the newest scientific thinking about our reality gives credence to what we call paranormal and in fact would define as normal.

Bad Mind offers the stories of experiencers in the continental U.S., the Hawaiian Islands, England, Caribbean islands, and India. The census is informal and unscientific but also "honest," to play off a phrase said by writer Robert Damon Schneck in a 2014 interview on Darkness Radio. Schneck said he believed if someone did an "honest census," going door to door asking people if they had had encounters with the supernatural, he believed many would say yes.

The collection ends with "A Visit to Usha's," an essay about my visit to Usha, a successful business woman, astrologer and intuitive who lives and works in Bangalore, India. Usha believes we in the East and the West are joining in a desire to understand our journeys. Usha collects rocks, not a common pursuit in India, and when I visited her home in Bangalore as we gazed at the rocks in glass cases Usha pulled the names of the rocks out of me like a shaman extracting trapped spirits. Her story provides an example of how a person can weave together seemingly disparate strands of life and maintain both an open spirit to unseen forces and success in the material world.

Why Can't We Think About Aliens?

originally published in *The Edge Magazine*,
September 2015

WE CAN THINK OF QUANTUM physics. For example, we've incorporated the phrase "quantum leap" into our everyday speech, as in "Our school made a quantum leap this year in math scores." We may not know the dictionary definition of quantum leap, which is the abrupt change of a particle from one state to another, but we know the term generally means something moved forward fast.

We can think of black holes. The term is used in astronomy and indicates a place in space with so much gravity pulling at its center than even light cannot get out. Anything that goes in will not come back out and will become as invisible as the black hole itself. As an example, consider money and people thrown at resource-sucking IT projects in the workplace. Despite black holes' invisibility, we don't need to see them to recognize a good metaphor.

We can even think of worm holes, imaginary extensions of black holes that theoretically would permit a person to time travel.

It is perfectly fine to discuss these scientific notions across all social stratums, our workplaces, places of worship, and on social media. You can do so without fear of your listeners rolling their eyes or sneering at you, unlike the experience of mentioning encounters with extraterrestrials or other anomalous beings. Here you must be cautious when publicly discussing. Apparently, it is fine to entertain the idea of something fantastical if it has a tie to science. Hitch your topic to science's rational-thought star, and it will get instant credibility.

Contrast that with public reception of topics that resist rational thought as a cognitive process to understand them: aliens or extraterrestrials, for example.

An audience member at a recent gathering of the Theosophical Society at Spirit United Church in Minneapolis got me thinking about this. "Why is it we can't think about extraterrestrials?" this fellow asked after he introduced himself to me during a break of the panel discussion. The panel was made up of four individuals, of which I was one, who had had encounters with anomalous beings. In UFO literature parlance, we were billed as "experiencers."

When we can't think about extraterrestrials, we are unable to weave them into our intellectual constructs with which we give our world meaning, such as spiritual philosophies or sociological theories. Unlike certain terms in quantum physics, our terms for extraterrestrials and other anomalous beings stand alone and unconnected, like language pariahs, unwanted and shunned. If these terms were members of a tribe, and if, say, our tribe had to escape the oncoming winter snows due to our flimsy animal skin outfits, like Sonny and Cher wore on their television program in the 1970s, the terms would be the sick, older members of the tribe. We would have to leave them behind because they'd slow us down and consume food and water needed for those who still had a chance.

Why does it seem thinking about extraterrestrials and all they evoke will use up all our oxygen? Why can't we think about aliens?

The audience member I spoke with uses the metaphor of astrology to explain what prevents us from thinking about aliens. "We can't use the Pluto energy [to think about extraterrestrials] because every time the topic comes up the energy is blocked," he said.

Pluto represents transformation and regeneration, often at the collective level. It is two-faced, however, and can also represent what Jungian and astrologer Gerry Goddard describes as the power of repression and destructive instincts and the "necessary restraints of collective interests."

To think of aliens is to think of the end of ourselves as we know us.

To think of aliens is to imagine a world where we as central thinkers no longer exist.

Perhaps blocked Pluto is a metaphor for the culture necessarily restraining us from thinking about aliens?

Is it perhaps not quite time for the end of us, or the "us" we have constructed?

These are questions without answers, rhetorical, as they say. They are questions I like to entertain when I'm not googling Sonny and Cher fur outfits.

ET in the Gulf
originally self-published as *Captain Chris* on amazon.com

CAPTAIN CHRIS STANDS AT THE helm of a boat in the Gulf of Mexico, scanning the pre-dawn sky. Chris, his real first name, 50, works for an oil company based in Houston, Texas, that manages oil rigs in the Gulf. It is not the oil company the U.S. government found responsible for the oil spill that occurred in the Gulf of Mexico in April 2010. It is another petroleum industry player which, like BP Oil, is in business partly to serve the needs of Americans such as myself who enjoy temperature control in our homes, offices, malls, churches and other structures in which we want to feel cool in summer and warm in winter.

All manner of beast in and on this body of water are still coming to terms with the effects of what is known as the

BP oil spill. The fires on that day in April 2010 have long been put out and much of the oil that arrived on nearby shores has been cleaned up. Those who have been found responsible are making costly reparations. Chris and the aquatic company he keeps, both human and non-human, are still recovering from the effects of the oil spill.

Chris keeps another type of company upon whom the effects of the oil spill may not be as evident, due to their more nebulous forms in our world: Unidentified Flying Objects (UFOs) and extraterrestrials. Chris has had a lifetime of encounters with mysterious craft and beings of anomalous origin.

Chris' encounters began with sightings of distant, mysterious lights moving erratically around the sky. He estimates he's seen over 300 crafts and lights of anomalous origin over his years of sightings. Over time his experiences have progressed to encounters with other-worldly beings.

Chris has experienced these encounters on land and on sea, as a child growing up in Gulf Breeze, Florida, and as an adult working in the Gulf; his encounters continue today in the Hill Country of Texas where he has lived since the BP oil spill and on the oil company boat on which he continues to work. Sometimes he is alone when these encounters occur, and sometimes others are with him. When there are multiple people involved in the encounter, they have functioned both as observers and active participants.

All in all, his encounters have been positive: "Throughout my life my encounters with these beings have always been good," Chris says.

As a boy growing up in Gulf Breeze in the 1960s and

Bad Mind

1970s Chris was interested in reptiles, especially snakes, which he and a couple of friends hunted in the woods near his home in Gulf Breeze. He and his friends fished in the bay between Gulf Breeze and Pensacola. He also helped his grandmother tend her garden. She introduced him to the care, feeding and lives of plants. Later, she would become his sole confidante when he began trying to make sense of his other-worldly encounters and the questioning about his world they seemed to force him into.

"[The UFO sightings] started in 1976 or 1977 when I was 12," Chris tells me. He and two others were fishing in the Pensacola waters when they witnessed a bright green UFO move across the sky from east to west. In about the same timeframe he experienced a ground-level encounter with an anomalous bright light in the woods between home and school and emerged with missing time and feeling emotionally affected.

Chris' boyhood love of fishing carried through into the 1980s when he was in his late teens and still living in Gulf Breeze.

"I saw the occasional anomalous light in the 1980s when I was fishing," Chris notes. "I saw them three or four times a year [in the 1990s], then a year or two with nothing. Then six or eight times a year."

Chris moved into adulthood, and in the 1990s began working for oil companies on their boats that tended the oil rigs in the Gulf of Mexico. His talents and skills seemed naturally to lead him to such a profession. "The only things I really excelled at were fishing, surfing and being on the water," Chris notes.

Chris was working on an oil company boat in the Gulf when the BP Oil Spill occurred in April 2010. His boat and those of other oil companies in the Gulf were sent in to assist.

When the methane gas expanded and rose into the BP rig, it exploded and burst into flames, engulfing the platform. One hundred and twenty-six crew members were aboard; before the platform sank two days after the explosion 94 crew members were rescued by helicopter and boat.

The fire burned for about two days. Oil continued to gush into the Gulf. In the end, the U.S. government estimated the total volume of leaked oil during the 87 days it flowed approximated 4.9 million barrels.

The BP company officials argue the government's figure doesn't account for the 810,000 barrels of oil that crews on Chris' boat and other oil company boats collected or burned.

Chris says the cleanup was just for show. "It did nothing. They covered it [the oil] up or sprayed it with chemicals. Only a minute amount of it was actually picked up. There's actually no way to pick up such huge amounts."

That April, while the Gulf burned, my priority was temperature control. I had left the warmth of Virginia for the frigidity of Minnesota. I must have heard news of the BP oil spill in the Gulf, but I don't recall fully taking it in. I'm smart and aware enough to have questioned BP's practices early on, when they and other petroleum companies began drilling for oil in the Gulf of Mexico. But I didn't. I didn't think to. When I thought of BP, I thought of the friendly green starburst and "BP" in yellow letters. I thought of gasoline to fill the tank of my car. I thought of warmth and light.

Chris was living in Houston at this time. He returned to his home there for his two-week respite from work on the boat, to his pool, the Mexican gang that lived next door and the two old Oak trees in the small, fenced-in yard.

At the end of each two-week furlough, Chris returned to the boat for two weeks of work. Close to the fires, the billions of gallons of gushing oil and what seemed the cosmetic nature of the cleanup he and others were assigned to do, he saw the gap between BP's public relation efforts to paint a positive picture of the recovery efforts and the reality of the situation.

"Seeing my Gulf destroyed about killed me," Chris says. "There were people who didn't give a rat's ass. Then there were those of us who cared deeply."

Like the dolphins and other marine life which inhabit the Gulf, Chris was deeply affected physically.

"It [the BP oil spill] messed with my brain," Chris says. "I often stop on words now and sometimes leave them out."

During this time Chris' mother bought a house on wooded acreage outside of Austin, Texas. Chris found solace there and soon left Houston for this refuge.

When Chris and his mother first moved onto the property, two members of a nearby monastery informed them their land had a vortex over it.

Shortly after Chris set out to find that vortex, letting his intuition guide him. It led him to a tree by a pond.

When Chris asked a visiting friend trained in working with subtle energies to locate the vortex, without knowledge of Chris' finding he too indicated the tree by the pond.

On Chris' next visit to the tree he brought along a Lemurian crystal he'd bought at a rock shop in California. This type of crystal has horizontal striations or grooves on the sides and is said to facilitate opening of consciousness. Chris sat down under the tree and placed the crystal on his forehead and, as he put it, "went into that zone." After meditating for some time,

> All of a sudden, I had a vision of this blue-skinned alien lady with curly hair pulled over in a bun. She was looking at me sideways like I wasn't doing something I was supposed to be doing or vice versa. I saw the mole on her cheek. Then I turned and 12 inches from me an alien gray was looking at me; we were studying each other. He had this really calm peaceful countenance on his wrinkles and his face. He seemed ancient, wise and good; like a good man. He had these big black eyes. He had wrinkles around his eyes and mouth. It was as though he'd been peaceful for a long time. He skin was like sharkskin, textured like that. We sat there for several seconds. I wonder if she [the blue lady] was like telling me you're fixing to meet someone.

Following this extraordinary encounter, in his customary rhythm Chris returned to the boat, his two weeks off complete.

Back on the boat, Chris' sightings of UFOs took a new turn: a syncing between his thoughts and their activity.

One night on the boat Chris watched a video of a psychic

predicting an event that would wipe out two-thirds of the earth's population.

> I was raw from that summer [after the April 2010 BP oil spill] and the video touched me deeply. Shortly after, I was running the boat south around four a.m. to a platform offshore when Orion was just coming up in the southeast. I connected with "them" in my mind and asked, if this planet becomes uninhabitable, are you guys taking us somewhere? Right when I thought that, a craft blinked in just to the left of Orion's belt, went across and blinked out, then did the same in reverse.

This syncing became tighter in the summer of 2014. Chris' thoughts and emotional states continued to yield a response from other-worldly entities but now their manifestation moved from distant lights to sentient beings.

"That summer," he notes, "I was seeing lots of crafts flying around us out here on the Gulf for several days in a row. I would see them almost every morning between three and five a.m." He is careful to draw a distinction between this activity and that of satellites: "They differ from satellites which you see out there. Satellites don't deviate from their course direction, speed or its brilliancy. The crafts vary in all those characteristics."

One night during Chris' overnight shift on the boat he sent out a mental request for communication from the other-worldly intelligence he suspected was behind the crafts' appearance. In response, a bronze mantid, or mantis, appeared in a vision and climbed aboard:

We were just sitting tied up on the buoy. It was a nice night with a nice breeze. I was in my hammock with the door to the wheelhouse open so I could keep an eye on the radar. I was just watching the sky and meditating when I saw more of the same. In a mildly irritated state I asked, "Can I please have some sort of communication other than watching you fly around up there?" I closed my eyes and calmed myself. Suddenly there was a strong yet subtle vision of a bronze-colored mantid set in a black background sort of looking sideways at me, visible from the shoulders up.

While looking at me sideways he came toward me slowly, and then that was it; he was gone. I said in my mind, "If that was real, give me something else." I got off the hammock and went and looked at my phone; it read 4:09 (like the cleaner). Then I went and looked at the electronics in the wheelhouse and they said the same time. So I went and laid back down on the hammock. A little breeze kicked up, and I looked back down at my phone and it said 3:23. I went back inside the wheelhouse, and the electronics in there said that time too. And then for some reason I thought of that time when I lost time in the fifth grade when the teacher said, "You can go now," and I had missing time between then and getting home. I wondered if that was like getting time back.

As Chris relates this encounter to me on the June 2015 morning of our interview, he says, "I wonder too if it was like a message saying, 'It's us.' It's a way of manipulating our reality and communicating with us. This is the way shamans communicate; it's not words; it's happenings."

Between October 2014 through December 2014, Chris began witnessing flashes low in the sky during his overnight stint at the helm. The unidentified sources flashed in ones, threes and sevens. Chris notes he didn't experience any particular emotional change or any other communication from these UFO flashes, "Except just more wonder."

> Sometimes I feel they were just sort of letting me know they're around, but who knows; I sure don't.
>
> It just seems to me that so many people are having these types of things happening. I just feel it [that something's up] in my heart.
>
> I'm not sure if people can take it in. For those of us who can what is our place in it? It seems like we're always forced to question. There's rarely an answer to things; there's just always just more looking around at things and thinking.

What Chris describes as "old knowledge" began pulling him as 2014 drew to a close. Chris notes in a personal communication on December 19, 2014, "I think there were times before when we knew who we were." Something ancient and wise was encompassing all aspects of his being—mind, body, what his senses apprehended, and the flashes from the UFOs and visions of other-worldly beings that synchronized to his thoughts and emotional states.

During part of that December's holidays Chris was at

home in the woods outside Austin. There he spent as much time as he could dwelling silently among the trees and plants of the property. The crafts' activity had waned, both before he had left the boat and now back home. He succumbed wholly, with mind, body and spirit, to the experience in the woods and the intelligence there he encountered among the trees and plants.

This two-week stint home, like all others, was restorative. However, he still felt deeply fatigued when he returned to the boat. "I am so very tired," he wrote after returning to the boat in January 2015.

Amidst struggling with his energy, his ability to sync with unseen forces continued to manifest. At the start of the new year while on the boat he began reading my account of my 30 years of encounters with anomalous beings. While reading certain parts he had powerful déjà vu. He had experiences that mirrored mine. About a month later, in February 2015, as he read the section titled "The Meaning" on his overnight shift, he looked to the north to see two bright stars sitting very close. After a few seconds they dimmed out together, exactly the same together. Thereafter, whenever Chris thought of my book, he saw a craft. They appeared to the north, the direction of my physical location. Chris describes the light coming from these craft as having a quality that is different.

"It was some connection with you there, with them," he says. "They were clearly telling me something about you, your book, and me."

Chris had to put down my recounting of my experiences from time to time while reading it, feeling overwhelmed by what it was evoking in him. Along with the pressures of his work he continued to contend with the ongoing physical effects after being in the Gulf during the BP Oil Spill. With work and these physical struggles, he continued to feel deeply tired and frazzled.

In July 2015, the blue lady again visited Chris and attempted to physically come on board the boat Chris captains. On that July night, Chris woke up just before 10 p.m. as he usually does to get on his midnight watch.

> I pulled out my Lemurian crystal and was listening to these little sounds called binaural beats that I listen to. These are different tones that supposedly put your mind in a certain mode. Some are peaceful, some give you energy. I held my crystal in my left hand. This is the same crystal I put on my forehead and then saw a blue alien lady.
>
> This night, I saw her in my mind and consciously connecting with her. This was 10 at night. You know what, I thought, maybe we could be friends with each other, help each other without enslaving each other. Is that possible? Can you appear here on this plane? I was saying these things mentally.
>
> I finished getting ready for my shift and went upstairs [on the boat for the hand-off with the captain finishing his shift]. One of the other captains was there, this older guy, 63 or so, who's from my hometown of Pensacola.
>
> "Chris," he said, "I'm going to tell you something. When I say this don't take it personally. Someone was

trying to get on board just now."

"What are you talking about?" I said.

The older captain said, "I heard a female voice in my head, 'Can I come through?'"

"What did you do?"

"I didn't let her through."

Without saying anything more, we did our hand-over, and he went downstairs.

I decided the next day to tell him what was going on that previous night.

After I told him, this old captain said, "I have these psychic abilities."

This was the first time he'd revealed this to me. He's real Christian right, Southern Baptist.

This old captain gets feelings that are acute. He doesn't get the exact visions so much. Maybe he's just more receptive to voices.

I have much sympathy for the old boat captain. Like him, I am a receiver without language to adequately express the gut feelings and random glimmerings I get. I bumble about and try to broach the subject with the human I think might be receptive to the information I seem to hold for them. I am like Rick Moranis' character in the Hollywood movie *Ghostbusters*, when he stumbles around New York City asking people in his path, "Are you Gozer?" This is the fate of us humans who by our nature are connected to the gods above and the dirt below but forever in between, straddling two worlds.

To Chris, it may be this quality that draws other-worldly

visitors to us:

> We humans have a wide variety of energies and things we can perceive and interact with. I think some of them [the visitors] have a narrow band what they can do; they're more of an energetic than a physical thing. I think that might be why we're so attractive to these beings.
>
> There's like two worlds we have to live in. We have to live in that world where we have to work, that materialistic world, and then to balance with this other world.

Finding that balance seems always to be our struggle in contemporary American life. This is a challenge unique to our times; 200 years ago, human lives ended on average at age 35. No wonder our ancestors dispensed with early Christian thinking that body and spirit were equally important and instead adopted the ancient Greek notion our bodies are split off from our spirits. Perhaps the only comfort was imagining that after a lifetime of following God's rule your spirit would ascend into the cool and bloodless celestial realms.

Like many of us, Chris must work at a job and pursue (or, in his case, be pursued by) an avocation, challenging him to hold the reins to his life's twin drivers lightly in his hands, to borrow a metaphor from James Reho in his article "When God is a Sheep in a Wolf's Clothing," published in the Summer 2015 issue of Parabola. To do so requires just absorbing what's around and within him, something

Chris notes people have been steered away from. Chris is aided in his task of holding the reins tethered to the twin streams that run through his life by the natural world and his relationship with it, which began in the woods around Gulf Breeze and in his grandmother's garden.

Over the past several years Chris has been exploring ways to more consciously contact non-human, energetic intelligence such as that emanating from plants.

> These past few years since the BP spill I've really been drawn more to plants. It's amazing how spiritual they are and how they want to help us. The Indians in South America know about this and have for thousands of years. The ancient Irish did too with their plant lore and belief that spirit was in all plant life. The book *Plant Spirit Medicine: The Healing Power of Plants*, by Eliot Cowan, talks about how the natives in southern countries use the ayahuasca plant to learn how to communicate with plants. In the ayahuasca visions the different plants come to them and tell them what they're for. The ayahuasca plant is the opening of communication to the plant world. The ayahuasca plant takes you to this world below the usual world.

Captain Chris' overnight shift at the helm of a boat in the Gulf of Mexico moved from darkness to light, and shortly he would guide the boat toward one of the oil platforms. Chris is never far away from the shores of home, where he grew up in Gulf Breeze and where he now lives in Texas, a half-circle of coast surrounding his Gulf. The snakes in

Bad Mind

Gulf Breeze rest easier now that he is grown, and only a few remember the boy and his friends who bicycled into the woods to hunt their kind. Outside Austin on several acres of wooded land, the plants and their spirits wait for rain and Chris.

Just Another Face of Spirit
originally published as
"Who Can Think About Aliens?"
in The Aquarian, Summer 2016

COULD COPERNICUS THINK ABOUT ALIENS? We don't know for sure, but we do know he could think about views that challenged those of his time and those held by the organization that both housed and employed him. He held the position of canon, a lay priest, with Frombork's cathedral in Torun, Poland, from the age of 21 until his death in 1543. When his duties allowed, he studied astronomy and wrote. The Church didn't approve of the 40-page book he wrote in about 1514 asserting the sun was the center of the universe; in fact, the Church deemed it heretical. However, the Church did not punish or persecute this part-time astronomer while he was alive.

Giordano Bruno could think about aliens. A philosopher and one-time priest in sixteenth century Italy, he wrote in his work *On the Infinite Universe and Worlds*, "Innumerable suns exist; innumerable earths revolve around these suns.... Living beings inhabit these worlds." Authorities from the Catholic Church brought charges against Bruno for the ideas expressed in his writing. After a seven-year imprisonment he was burned alive at the stake in 1600.

Like Copernicus, retired McGill University professor Don Donderi, Ph.D., was able to study his side interests within the protection of an established institution. While Donderi was in his tenured, academic position at McGill University he was able to study alien abductions during the period 1962 – 2009 without threats to his career. He notes in a February 25, 2013, *National Post* article, "I had tenure. I could study things without worrying about what other people thought about them. This is a very liberating thing." He also notes in the article, "I've been on the mainstream of science and engineering my entire professional life." Donderi's book, *UFOs, ETs and Alien Abductions: A Scientist Looks at the Evidence*, came out in 2013, after he had retired from his academic post.

Don Donderi can think about aliens, and as a result of his work he is helping many of us begin to think about them too.

John E. Mack, Harvard professor and psychiatrist, learned to think about aliens. He counseled individuals who believed they had been abducted by extraterrestrials. After the 1994 publication of his best-selling book, *Abduction:*

Human Encounters with Aliens, his Harvard colleagues demanded an investigation into his work. After 14 months the investigating committee declined to take any action; they did not uncover anything in the way of professional misconduct.

John Mack's colleagues definitely could not think about aliens.

What is it about extraterrestrials that makes it so hard for us to think about them?

Two hundred years ago we couldn't think of stones falling from the sky as real. We considered them folk tales. Today we call those falling stones meteorites. Perhaps one day we will look back at our inability to think about aliens in a similar way, as a mental quirk from a more innocent time.

When American filmmakers think about aliens or the other-worldly beings many of us have encountered, they dramatize them in a cartoonish fashion: for example, the "grays," the little gray-skinned fellows often outfitted in work overalls; "Nordics," tall, blonde, attractive individuals apparently of Scandinavian descent dressed in white flowing robes whose gracious social skills hint at having attended alien charm school, also known to be of kind intent toward the humans; and the Reptilian aliens, aka lizard men, known to be cunning, shape-shifting and evil. Not surprisingly the blonde and white-skinned Nordics are pure and good, and the dark and scaly Reptilians are wily and bad.

These representations of other-worldly beings are likely too extreme for most of us to incorporate into our thinking. They are embedded in entertainment. We don't incorporate Disney characters into our thinking other than to acknowledge them as cultural icons; why, then, would we incorporate film versions of other-worldly beings into our thinking? We are further hindered by our habit of rational thought and the split from imaginal thought. Without the ability to engage in imaginal thought, we cannot find where other-worldly beings fit in the fabric of our lives, past and present.

How do we recover that ability in ourselves to think with the parts of our brains and minds that allow us to enter into the imaginal realms John Mack speaks of? How do we recover our ability to think about what we term aliens and begin to see them as Choctaw nation member Sequoyah Trueblood describes his alien visitors "just one 'face of spirit'"?

Jungian analyst and astute cultural observer Llorraine Neithardt says we have to "expand the image" when colossal change confronts us. The need to tackle such a task lies at the root of why we don't like change and resist it.

How do we expand the image of what we say is real?

By employing active imagination, we may be able to create a sort of imaginal grove where the extraordinary can live and evolve. Sonu Shamdasani writes in the introduction to *The Red Book* that Jung's active imagination procedure involved "deliberately evoking a fantasy in a waking state, and then entering into it as into a drama."

Perhaps there we can learn to think about aliens as just another face of spirit.

My Journey Through Stupid Times

WHEN I WAS 10 YEARS old, I lived with my family on the Marine Corps Air Base or MCAS in Yuma, Arizona. My dad's tour of duty on an aircraft carrier off the coast of Vietnam had ended. Instead of running air ops he was now an air traffic controller on the base.

Before movies began at the base theater, we rose and stood with our hands on our hearts when the Star-Spangled Banner was played. We swam in the officer's pool and got in trouble with the Military Police or MPs when they caught us playing in underground bunkers in a restricted area near the desert edge of the base. My younger brother faked crying, and the MP let us go with a warning. The hymnals in the base church substituted militaristic terminology in some of the hymns. I blithely sang of Christ's super-sonic jets, imagining my dad directing them from the air-traffic control tower, as I watched the Timberlake boys in the front pew. The Timberlake boys and their parents lived down the street from us in base housing identical to ours. The Timberlake boys were too young for me but not my older sister.

I read from my white leather-bound Bible to my two younger sisters most nights, their bedtime story. I'm not sure why I chose the Bible to read from; we weren't a particularly religious family. We attended services regularly on whatever base we were stationed at, adopting whatever denomination it happened to be. Church was a part of our life but not oppressively so. I had earned my Bible by memorizing all the books of the Bible and reciting them one Sunday morning in the base chapel in front of the entire congregation. I liked going to church at the Yuma base chapel. The Timberlake boys and their parents filled a pew, and we sat several rows behind them. I liked to observe the Timberlake boys—Bill, Robert and Paul. There was something very enticing about all that male energy. At the time I didn't understand the concept of intuition, but that's what allowed me to sense that the Timberlake boys seemed to vibrate with a certain energy, in particular the oldest, Bill. At 18 he was handsome and confident in a Tom Jones' way.

When I read the books of the Old Testament aloud to my younger sisters, I envisioned an early world where God's people had to battle demonic beings in order to make the world safe and humane. There seemed to be a lot of unfair rules for women all due to the behavior of a few notables, e.g., Jezebel, who went about enticing the men with their feminine ways.

Bad Mind

I don't recall being horrified by the diligence and violence with which the new religious order, Christianity, erased those of the old ways. The Old Testament world was far removed from mine, and existed in a two-dimensional way, rather than a fully-realized world. I was a child with imagination and rich interior life. Given the family I was born into, I adopted the rules for what was tolerated and what was demonstrated and fit my imaginings to those rules.

When my encounters with other-worldly beings began in 1968 after we had moved to the dark woods of Minnesota, I began telling myself stories during the day. One of my favorites was one in which a girl came from ancient times into our modern world. She would be bewildered, and I would have to explain what certain things were and how they worked, light switches, traffic and shoes. She looked like a contemporary girl of that time, the late 1960s—pixie haircut, blonde, slender. That was probably so she could blend in with just an outfit change from my closet.

Though I couldn't articulate it at the time, I knew there was a rule that prohibited talking about fantasy stories I told myself during the day and frightening visits from other-worldly entities at night. I feared breaking that rule. I had observed what happened to girls who let slip details of anything that should remain secret, such as a belief in ghosts. Other girls (and boys) labeled them ditzes. I feared that power.

This is generally a good way to keep a girl (and boy) in line. Once upon a time we did this with gruesome fairy tales. We—speaking of humans in general—also once did this with the threat of charges of heresy and punishment by death, often carried out on individuals just so you knew we meant business.

When I attended college in the early 1980s living in the Norfolk / Virginia Beach area of Virginia, I learned facts about the world that changed how I thought and lived. I became educated about the many inequities in our world, particularly in the lives of women and people of color. I researched and wrote about the women healers in Europe in the middle ages who were branded and burned as witches. I discovered most of the world was without safe drinking water. I read about the women who fed their babies Nestle formula and blamed the babies' death on themselves when the formula could not sustain those new lives. I marched on Washington to protest the possibility of nuclear war and volunteered for writing campaigns supporting women's rights. I began to craft an identity separate from what you might call "mainstream" America: the folks who watched T.V., shopped recreationally and went through life without much thought to inequities and our overflowing landfills.

It was not until I cried out for paper products in Bangalore, India, that I realized just how mainstream America I was. Stopped in traffic on the way from the airport to St. Mark's, our hotel in Bangalore, I watched a man in a loin cloth and turban walking among the stopped automobiles, auto-rickshaws and motor bikes waving his wares — rolls of paper towels. I had no idea the rarity he was offering. At the hotel, I requested tissues at the front desk. I anticipated a big box of facial tissues like we have at home; you know, Kleenex, and when the kindly hotel worker handed me a pocket-size package of 10 tissues, I could only stare dumbfoundedly at the packet and the 10 tissues I would have to make last for two weeks. A local yoga teacher graciously invited me into his home and yoga shriya or studio where I was to take a class with him and his wife. The taxi driver waited for me, parked in front of the yoga teacher's house for several hours. Before the class I used the yoga teacher's bathroom, unattached to the house and his yoga shriya. When I reached for the toilet paper but found none, and never would, I came to a new understanding about myself. There was no way I could reframe this. I was an American through and through, defined by my love of paper products. My people. I had more in common with fans of the Kardashians than those of the *PBS NewsHour*.

Given who I am, my upbringing and my cultural heritage I had several scrims to pull back before I could see the reality of other, invisible worlds and the beings who inhabit them besides our own and humans in it. I am still easily stumped by what the other-worldly beings want to give me. John E. Mack, a Harvard psychiatrist who could think about aliens, relates the story of South African medicine man Credo Mutwa telling him, "I just get mad... because this thing is real. I just get furious because the people from the stars are trying to give us knowledge, but we are too stupid." It's kind of him to use the royal we, though I suspect he can think about aliens and what they are offering us. It is people like me who are too stupid.

Is there a source for my stupidity? Some say it is the divisions my western thinking draws between mind and spirit. This shows up in the divided way we describe our thinking: for example, right brain / left brain; analytic vs. intuitive; brain people and heart people. All mean basically the same thing: I shutter myself with blinders of rational thought and effectively shut out entire worlds, not only the invisible worlds but the one we humans all participate in on this planet, what we agree is our daily reality. This is how I compartmentalize such events as the April 2010 BP oil spill and my 30 years of encounters with beings from other worlds. I'm not proud of this ability but at this late date in my life can admit to it with the hope of finding a different way.

You may not have layers to peel back before you can see other realities. If that is the case, I applaud you. How can I support you? In the meantime, I will also support those individuals who are like me, a bit blockheaded when it comes to taking in other realities and the beings who inhabit them. I will stumble and bumble my way through understanding and articulating the true nature of another being, whether that being is kith, kin or extraterrestrial. I will learn to think about aliens. I will come to understand their nature and where our encounters with them fit into our daily lives, our culture, our history. I will weave them back into the fabric of my life.

The central problem with not being able to think about aliens is who is defining what is respectable and acceptable to think about. Pinpoint who is behind that and examine their language for describing the world, what is considered real about it and how they respond to others who question that reality. Then you might see why the English language lacks words and expressions and even images that reflect

Bad Mind

the other worlds that surround us.

Bad Mind
originally published as "99 Obeah-men" in Akashic
Books' Duppy Thursday series short fiction,
April 6, 2017

I WAS THIN, BLONDE AND ignorant of how little it takes to make mean girls hate you. I thought knowledge of my encounters with beings from the spirit-world would incur their wrath; accordingly, I kept those experiences secret from the time they began when I was 10. The encounters began innocently with a space-boy named Eric who took me on tours of the universe in his Jetson-style spaceship with its bubble on top that allowed us a panoramic view. They progressed to long sessions with machine-like extraterrestrials sitting across from me at a table and transmitting telepathic messages into my mind. A Man in Black paid a waking-time visit to me, and, once, frogs rose up from below deep winter snows to rain on me and my sister Barbara. Over time, I came to assist the extraterrestrials in their metamorphosis from their world to ours. During this phase objects from their world began to manifest in my waking world. At the same time, I began experiencing physical invisibility and seemed to be under new laws of physics—what had once seemed solid now seemed to be vibrations. All the while, I kept those experiences a secret. I had seen early on how mean girls targeted freaky girls for ridicule and shunning. In truth, many in mainstream America did the same thing, but I was more frightened of mean girls. They had the power to make other girls' lives miserable. I thought keeping my strange encounters a secret would keep me safe; how misinformed and innocent I was! All it really took was to shine a little more brightly.

The opening salvo in what became my co-worker's imaginary war started when I brought a picture of my wedding gown into the office. It lay flat on my desk, facing me, in a fan with other miscellaneous office papers. My co-worker Emily came in, sat down at the chair across from my desk and immediately noticed the photo. She leaned in to get a closer look at the satin slip dress. "Designer?" she asked. Her tone was cool, but I knew those metallic notes: envy coated in anger with thoughts of retribution.

"Yes," I said, "Vera Wang." I wasn't normally a name-dropper; however, I was emboldened by the beauty of the dress, my happiness at getting married, and the novelty of taking part in a conversation about wedding details, something thousands of women take for granted. I was 47 and old for a first-time American bride.

Emily looked at me, her eyes narrowing to vaporize, like an alien robot shooting laser beams from her eyes. "That shouldn't be your wedding dress," she said. "It should be my friend Sarah's."

At that time, in 2006, the average marrying age for a woman in the United States was 27. I didn't need statistics to tell me this; I'd spent plenty of money on wedding gifts not only for my friends and acquaintances but recently for their children as they became of age and began to do statistically relevant things. I'd neither wed nor bred in those 20 years. I had worked, but that didn't give me a count in anything particularly relevant except the hoi polloi. If I'd been brave enough, I would have called myself a spinster in Mary Daly's definition of the word: "A 'spinster' is a woman who spins, who creates, who goes off on her own." I created and went off on my own but had to work a lot to finance my figurative spinning. I had a full-time day job and often took additional part-time work at night and on weekends. Someone had asked me recently, "So you never married?" With one foot in the crypt, apparently, how could I be a threat to anyone? I imagined pity, not envy, from the women who ran the Big Girls' Clubs such as my 28-year-old co-worker Emily who was married with several children.

As a teenager I had learned to avoid the wrath of girls like Emily, pretty, clear-skinned, outgoing, and always scanning the horizon for new territory to conquer. I shunned makeup, wore clothing certain not to emphasize my curves, and kept my bright plans for finding my way and making my mark in the world to myself. In this way I hoped to show I was one step down from those scary girls, not a threat and therefore not a target. I kept my encounters with beings from the spirit world a secret. If those girls knew of these and my secret life stream in which they existed, they and their ilk would brand me a freak.

Planning my wedding, I felt brazen. My ovaries were shrinking to the size of raisins; a pregnancy scare a few years before had turned out to be perimenopause. My would-be inseminator, who liked silence even more than I did, had asked me to marry him. It seemed I had a shot at engaging in one of the two most relevant activities for women in our American culture (my raisin-sized ovaries would preclude the other).

Shortly after Emily icily informed me my dress should have been her friend's, she went to a manager in our group and said I was causing a hostile work environment. As a result, I was demoted.

My Caribbean friend Matthew tells me in his part of the world, the island of Antigua, this is called being "bad minded." When you are afflicted with bad mind, you feel envious of someone else's good fortune and believe it should be yours, not theirs, or believe whatever boon has come into their life should belong to you or someone you know. When you are bad minded, the feelings are strong and may cause you to work to bring misfortune down upon the person whose good fortune you covet.

When I told Matthew my story of my-coworker's response to the photo of my wedding dress, he nodded, unsurprised.

"People will do black magic on you just because they think that you are happier than them," says Matthew. "Jealousy is a very, very strong thing that drives a lot of people to do odd things."

Bad Mind

Matthew is smart and articulate, and his voice lilts in the island's musical cadence and word choice.

Those with bad mind go under cover of darkness to the Obeah-men, men and women who practice black magic, and ask them to put a spell on their target.

We might use the verb "cast," but Matthew's choice of "put" signals the everyday nature of spellcasting on the island.

Once you pay the Obeah-men to work a spell, they are working on someone, according to Matthew.

"In the island... it's hard to point the finger," Matthew tells me, using a different preposition than we might use. "It's hard to know [who is behind the spell]. You will not know where it's coming from."

In contrast, as Matthew notes, with a nod to my disgruntled coworker, in the U.S. we have at our disposal the ability to identify who might be wishing us ill or who we have offended and therefore who is likely to be behind the stroke or strokes of bad fortune that befall us.

How true! When I was ninth grade, if you found your bra frozen in the freezer the morning after a slumber party, it wouldn't be long before the snickering told you who was behind it. If the girls on the bus to band camp wanted to let you know you were a nothing in their eyes, they made a show of shunning you, pretending you didn't exist. A girl could also steal another girl's boyfriend, but I never had boyfriends in junior high or high school, so that was a form of bad-mind revenge I never experienced.

Matthew also notes that in contrast to Antigua and other Caribbean countries in America we have no one to go to get protection. On Antigua people may obtain protection from Obeah-man or their parish priest. The parish priest will perform blessings on parishioners' houses, cars and any material acquisition that could cause bad mind in others.

Matthew explains, "People might say, 'Oh, you got a new car, you think you're moving up.' Blessing the car is done to protect it from that bad mind."

This is the same with houses. "People having the bad mind, they see you stepping up in life, you built a house and they might want to send demons to try and play with you," Matthew says.

To protect his home from demons, playful or otherwise, Matthew asked his parish priest to bless the new house he had built for his family.

"He prays, and he sprinkles holy water and he signs the cross on every door post, blessing the house and the land it is on," Matthew says.

People on Antigua also commonly go to an Obeah-man to get trinkets, rings and bracelets loaded up with protection. "Loaded up" is the term Matthew uses, conjuring an image of powerful protection embedded in the jewelry. People carry these protective items with them to ward off incoming curses as well as lessen the power of those that have already found their way in. The loaded-up bracelet keeps evil at bay, and the trinket protects family. The ring will warn you.

"If any harm is coming your way, it [the ring] will start to burn your finger," Matthew explains.

It never occurred to me to tie my misfortune to the possibility of a bad-minded co-worker nor did it occur to me to protect myself from incoming curses. Such thinking would imply a pipeline between invisible and visible worlds. I grew up in an American culture that said that pipeline didn't exist, nor did the supernatural beings which consorted with the humans who functioned as intermediaries or gateways between the two worlds.

In a fit of mind bad, our European forebears who came to this country and claimed it as theirs swept the original heirs and their beliefs out of the way and at the same time hoped to render the inhabitants of the invisible spirit world non-existent. For two hundred years those who shaped the belief in what our American culture stands for taught us we should ignore that world and its power. If we have encounters with beings from that world, we should assume we are imagining them. Our cultural leaders have done a thorough job of convincing us of this; it is rare to encounter anyone in this culture who understands the nature and reality of spirit-world or anomalous beings (e.g., extraterrestrials, demons) and accepts them as a normal part of everyday living.

Ethnologist Holger Kalweit writes in *Dreamtime and Inner Space: The World of the Shaman*, "Only a few of us who live in modern Western civilization understand that benevolent 'helping spirits' and 'imaginary friends' are by no means projections of an imagination gone riot."

Some of the original folk of this country believed in an inhabited spirit world that existed alongside this daily life we call reality. This invisible world was peopled by powerful, supernatural beings. To hear one of them whisper in your ear was a good and natural thing; it might also mean you were marked for a special role which you grew into with the right training and powers.

When our European forebears arrived on America's shores the burning times had just begun in Europe. Though the Catholic Church primarily targeted individuals they labeled heretics for suggesting beliefs that ran counter to the Church's, they also extended their methods to the women healers they branded witches. The Church burned many of these individuals alive at the stake. The women, often without means but possessors of knowledge of healing plants, were accused of consorting with invisible beings. The European women accused of witchcraft and their knowledge of healing herbs were useful until the male medical profession began to grow. Then they became threats, daring to practice medicine, as one court transcript put it, which necessitated their burning, a rather violent form of unfriending. Once the original folk in what we call America had fulfilled their usefulness, for example, helping the newcomers master a winter or two, our European forebears would build the country on their blood and bones but certainly not their beliefs. As hard as they tried, however, they could not make the spirit-world and its inhabitants go away. Those beings didn't give up on us, even though our American culture said they didn't exist and, further, said anyone who spoke openly about such encounters and the beings as real was nutty and perhaps delusional. They and their stories were to be discounted, considered myth but not reality. If you had these encounters and if you were wise to the ways of American culture, you didn't speak of them. You probably assumed they couldn't possibly be real.

Bad Mind

I doubted the reality of the beings I encountered over my 30 years of experiences with extraterrestrials, Men in Black, demons, angels, bronze giants, something that called itself an Endoform and inhabitants of the spirit world. More accurately, my rational mind held this doubt, and I tried to let my rational mind guide me through understanding my encounters with the extraordinary. This was a losing strategy. "You assume that [the rational mind] gives you the truth," writes Anne Lamott in *Bird by Bird,* "because the rational mind is the golden calf this culture worships, but this is not true." At the same time, no doubt a result of rational mind, I feared ridicule or worse should I speak openly about this large and secret part of my life. I kept silent and shunted the inhabitants of the other worlds who visited me into a separate life stream, Life Stream Two, so Girl in Life Stream One could live what we think of as a "normal" life, one that includes work, friends, love and social acceptance, all signs you are part of the tribe.

I could only tell my story when I had lost my place in the tribe of the American corporate worker. Thank you, bad-minded Emily, for setting that in motion; you set me free.

In our and other western countries it seems we require dramatic losses and epiphanies to remember who we once were.

Grief can serve to sufficiently reduce us. Linda, from Birmingham, England, now in her 40s, experienced the out-of-body phenomena when she was 17 years old during a time of family loss and grieving. Her maternal Grandfather had died, and Linda was profoundly affected.

"I felt the grief and emotion of everyone in the family,"

she writes. "I soaked it up like a sponge."

In her grief, she developed insomnia. On about the fourth night of it she recalls,

> I was lying on my back and suddenly had the sensation that my body felt lighter and I could not feel the bed beneath me. I was not alarmed by this and actually felt quite calm and relaxed – I had not felt this good for a while. Very slowly and gently I felt as if I was levitating upwards towards the ceiling. I felt wonderful – floating horizontally with my nose only a couple of inches from the hard surface. How I did it I do not know, but I slowly turned over so I had my back to the ceiling. I looked down and saw myself lying on my back on the bed; my eyes were closed, and I looked very pale but peaceful. It was then I noticed the silver thread; it protruded from my stomach and my eyes followed its length down to my body on the bed where it was attached like an umbilical cord.
>
> I felt immediate panic and heard the rushing sound in my ears as I instantly felt myself very quickly falling away from the ceiling back towards my bed. I landed with a jolt and lay there on my back and stared at the ceiling as if nothing had happened.

Linda notes the insomnia continued for some time, though she experienced being out of body only this once (so far; Linda still walks this earth).

Linda rarely speaks of the experience, and even now, many years later, is wary of giving it a place in reality or the fabric of her life or world she lives in: "How and why did this experience occur? Was I hallucinating through lack of sleep, or did my soul temporarily leave my body? I have had no further experiences such as this."

Fear of our western forefather's bad mind is strong. It keeps our stories in check. We tell only those that reflect how acceptable we are and how well we fit in. Our hidden stories are heavy, and we, solitary soldiers, learn to shoulder that burden early on.

On Matthew's island people stay cocooned in the beliefs of their culture. When islanders encounter anomalous beings, either other-worldly companions existing side by side or more malevolent forces sent by jealous others to cause problems, they have a place in their culture to hang their hat, to see where their experience fits in. Whatever cocoon we may have once had that provided a societal cushion between ourselves and the unknown outer world might be too far back in our history to reach. According to Merlin Stone in *When God Was a Woman*, that began in about 2400 AD when waves of invasion by northern tribes toppled the Goddess and ended the clan way of life. We've been fending for ourselves for a long time.

Clanless, how can we safely tell the truth of who we are? What protection is available to us in the absence of rings and trinkets loaded up with protection?

We can learn from those cultures and sub-cultures that acknowledge a world full of mostly invisible beings living side by side with us. There are cultures like Matthew's where these beliefs are common and widespread. Then there are cultures like Linda's England and my America where many of us go underground with our other-worldly experiences. After I outed myself in 2014, it seemed everyone I met had a story to tell; many had never told anyone out of fear of ridicule and loss of friends, family and job. Something key is happening to us, and I write those individuals' stories so we may understand what life looks like when you have one foot in the spirit world and the other in what we call reality. With time, we can learn from each other's missteps and other cultures which never stopped believing in the spirit world.

From Matthew's island home of Antigua comes a cautionary tale from which we might take a few suggestions.

In Pickets Village there was a gravedigger. He was known to the people in the village as an undertaker, but his main job was to dig graves. He also served the people who worked black magic. They could command him to go about the village and take people's clothing. The people of power needed these personal items to work their black magic on their target.

At this time, shortly before Matthew was born, certain people of power on the island were trying to get his grandmother. They sent the undertaker to find personal items of Matthew's grandmother. He found the family's house and clothesline, but he picked the wrong set of underwear from the line.

He took the underwear, which actually belonged to Matthew's aunt, back to those who had commanded him to retrieve it. They put a spell on it, and the undertaker put it on a body in the cemetery that was starting to rot.

As the corpse continued to rot, the living person whose

intimate pieces of clothing now adorned the corpse started to decay from the inside as well.

Matthew's aunt, a heavy woman, or "fairly thick" as Matthew puts it, from what he saw in family pictures, began to get small. Over the course of about four months she withered away from the inside out. She didn't have any scars or blemishes on the outside, Matthew notes; her skin didn't change. Her body just started to shrink. She got smaller and smaller until she just died.

"She died the October before I was born in December," Matthew says.

Since that time Matthew notes the island people don't leave clothing overnight anymore. They still hang their wash on the outside lines; at that time people did not have washers and dryers, and this is still true today.

Even in a place with potent options available to protect one's self, there are still people of such power who, if consulted, can kill you.

Bring your underwear in from the line before the sun sets. Consider the degree to which you reveal your vulnerabilities and instead offer those tender aspects greater protection. Refrain from public display of your designer wedding gown. Acknowledge the envy that resides in most of us, betraying our needing, wanting, insecure selves. Most of us are a phrase or image away from bad mind, when our grasping, envious natures are evoked. It may not take much to stir this up in those around you and an accompanying desire to bring you down. Unwittingly, I made it easy for someone with bad mind to find what they needed to make me suffer.

Stoke not the smoking logs of the fire waiting to rage.

An Old-Fashioned Fairy

AMITY IS 63 AND LIVES and plans to die on the north shore of Oahu. Her twin diagnoses, end-stage liver disease and cancer, have freed her. She is shedding certain trappings of her earthly life: jewelry, clothing, secrets. She has come to me with tales of her other-worldly encounters.

Like most experiencers, just talking about her encounters is a major step. To do so breaks an American taboo: speaking openly of personal spirit-world encounters. Taboos help to keep us in line and hold our shared worldview together. If you break the taboo, others might feel threatened. Crush the worldview, crush the person, to paraphrase John E. Mack.

I knew Amity once, years ago. We both lived in Tuscaloosa, Alabama. Then, she didn't speak of her other-worldly encounters, nor I mine. We were both young, hopeful and unencumbered by the weight of time, loss and regrets. Maybe we both needed that weight to feel sufficiently grounded to come out about our secret experiences.

Amity's first encounter of two occurred in 1974 in rural Alabama, near the Georgia border.

> I encountered a UFO along with a group of friends on a weekend in 1974. We'd all gotten together in a friend's house on the edge of pasture in Crawford, Alabama, a small town near the Georgia border, not far from the Army post Fort Benning in Columbus, Georgia. I was 21. We'd all known each other since high school. Jim, my first husband, was there, along with four other married couples and another friend. Several were brothers.
>
> I was in the living room, and the others, including my husband were in the kitchen. Suddenly their voices raised in excitement, shouting about lights. I heard the commotion as they ran to the screen door of the kitchen.
>
> I held back. I had never heard Jim and our friends sound as they did; they sounded excited in a way I'd never heard humans sound before. Everyone was sober; none of us had been drinking or imbibing in anything that might have impaired our perceptions.
>
> Finally, I rose and went into the kitchen. Everyone was making their way out the screen door. Eventually I followed.
>
> A giant disc with multi-colored lights like Christmas lights sat on the ground in the large pasture behind the house. I could see the outer surface of the craft looked like old, gray metal. It was absurd how much it

looked like the spaceships on television shows.

Jim started to run toward the landed craft.

I thought, "I want nothing to do with this," and in that the second the multi-colored lights on the craft began to spin, and the craft lifted up and out of the pasture.

I asked Amity how the encounter affected her, her husband and her friends. This had become a pivotal question for me when interviewing experiencers. So far I'd found most people who'd encountered something other-worldly or extraordinary stayed in the stage of awe when they recollected the experience. Few attempted to understand how and in what way it had changed them.

Amity responded, "I tend to just accept the reality of [my encounters] without question or doubt then disengage from the energy. For whatever reason it just leaves me alone. Even at age 21, I felt it left me alone, the flying saucer, that is, because I believed it, respected it, the experience, but wished to stay in my own realm and leave it to its."

She had a similar response when she encountered fairies in a friend's home on Big Island 29 years later in 2003. In her second marriage she had traveled to Hawaii in failing health after being diagnosed with Hepatitis C the previous year. Alone in her friend Cindy's home in the middle of the rain forest on Big Island, she observed the fairies' fluttering energy in the pitched roof above her friend's bed:

> The rafters of the ceiling rose to a peak over Cindy's bedroom. That's where the energy was; right over

> the bed, right over Cindy's bedroom. I could feel that peak had an unusual energy. It was movement and it was feeling.
>
> I felt the fluttering in the rafters above me. I knew there was some energy up there. I felt it for hours.
>
> I thought, that sounds like something to me, but I don't see anything. I might just want to leave it alone. I decided it didn't feel threatening.
>
> It happened every night for seven nights. The fluttering presence manifested only after dark.

As it turned out, the Big Kahunas had recently blessed the home following poltergeist activity. Amity learned this when she spoke to her friend Cindy on the phone during the visit. Cindy was not surprised to hear Amity had sensed fairies. The Kahunas believed the fairies moved in following the blessing to continue protecting Cindy's home.

Amity let the fairies be, not trying to own them or the experience. Like an old-fashioned fairy, Amity could engage then disengage with the energy around her. Her features were even fairy-like: high, prominent cheekbones, upturned eyes, fine hair that lay close to her skull.

Perhaps the ability to psychologically separate is the necessary quality for encounters with other-worldly beings. It seems to allow an entrance for energies and beings out of our daily world. Amity seems at peace with this quality in herself. I have always been uncomfortable with it in myself. For me and for Amity, our bodies then our lives had to falter before we could think intelligently about our other-worldly visitors and the worlds in which they exist.

I Dream of Djinni
originally published in The Aquarian, Spring 2017

WHEN I WAS 10, I desperately wanted Major Tony Nelson to ask Jeannie to marry him. Could he not see how his captive genie was so right for him? She knew it; we young girls in their television audience knew it. Why was it taking him so long to see it?

The American sitcom "I Dream of Jeannie" which ran from 1965 to 1970 taught me gentlemen wait. It also taught me genies are blonde and curvy and obey whoever uncorked their bottle. By the time I learned about the original genies, the Jinn, I couldn't appreciate the fear and awe they invoke in those who believe in them. A pal of mine from Pakistan, now living in the US, tells me, "Some people will give their soul to have the earthly goods the Jinn can offer."

In Hollywood's version you need only uncork the genie's bottle. In "I Dream of Jeannie" Major Anthony (Tony) Nelson finds a bottle on the beach near where his one-man spacecraft has landed in the South Pacific. He uncorks the bottle and by doing so becomes Jeannie's master. More often than not he forbids her from using her powers. As far I know Major Nelson didn't have to give his soul to enjoy the earthly goods Jeannie offered, though I like to think he gave his heart when the two eventually married in season five.

The Jinn are said to be able to take on human form and tempt humans with gifts and riches. So could Jeannie. The Jinn are supernatural beings who can grant wishes and curses. Jeannie too! The Jinn rank lower than angels but higher than humans. Here our genies part ways. Jeannie called Major Nelson "master," making her subservient status clear. As a genie, in Hollywood, anyway, she was below humans on the status ladder. She would have to clear a very big hurdle to get any closer to the angels supposedly above humans.

Jeannie didn't start out as a genie; a Blue Djinn turned her into one. The Jinn also didn't start out as genies; they weren't always supernatural troublemakers. Early on, in their angelic form, they were acknowledged to exist in a realm between humans and the divine. That intermediate realm was (is) as real and objective as ours, according to Sorbonne professor Henry Corbin in his book *Creative Imagination in the Sufism of Ibn 'Arabi* (translated from the French by Ralph Manheim, Princeton University Press, Bollingen Series XCI, 1969).

Major Nelson is kind of like Ibn 'Arabi, a mystic born in 13th century Spain who explored this intermediate realm. Ibn 'Arabi encountered beings from that realm a little earlier than Major Nelson, and Ibn 'Arabi's life's work would demonstrate that direct line to the divine. He was influenced by both Plato, ancient Greek philosopher, and Avicenna, an Islam thought-leader who lived in Spain about a hundred years before Ibn 'Arabi. Avicenna was a physician and philosopher whose thinking was aligned with Plato's and reconciled the rational with the mystical; both the mundane and the transcendent had a place in his cosmology. At that time, due to Avicenna's influence, so did Islam.

In Avicenna's belief system, angels inhabited an intermediate realm between the earthly and the divine. Humans could access this realm directly, without an intermediary, but not by using the sense organs. Sight, hearing, taste, touch, and smell would be of no use in attempting to perceive the angels and cipher their symbology. Instead, humans must use a function called active Imagination, according to Corbin. Imagination, he explains, is "correlated with a universe peculiar to it, a universe endowed with a perfectly 'objective' existence and perceived precisely through the Imagination." This universe was that of the angels. To connect directly with it, humans must quiet the rational mind and employ active Imagination, and then the angels' divine mysteries would become known to them. Ibn 'Arabi fully embraced this belief; he easily accessed the intermediate realm. Through his personal experiences and his writing, the esoteric tradition of Islam found its full expression.

At this time in medieval Europe, Islamic and Christian communities lived in close proximity; the members of these two groups "communicated their philosophies to one another," writes Corbin. In Ibn 'Arabi's time, the Christian religious leaders and academics were attempting to reconcile the philosophy of the ancient philosophers, namely Plato and Aristotle, with Christian theology. These leaders and scholars were, according to Corbin, gripped by "fear of the Angel" and they harshly criticized Avicenna's philosophy and, by extension, Ibn 'Arabi's developing school of mystical thought. These church authorities and academics warmed much more easily to the ideas of another Islam thought leader and contemporary of Ibn 'Arabi's and friend of his father's: Averroes.

In comparison to Avicenna's focus on theories and ideals, considered to be a Platonic approach, Averroes' focused on the more practical and rational, considered to be an Aristotelian approach. Humans had no touch of divinity and varied in their ability to apprehend the divine; in fact, some might not have the ability at all. To get an audience with the divine, the deficient humans would need a go-between, someone ordained with spiritual authority by an official body of believers. In general, though, Averroes' approach was considered to be based on Aristotelian logic, and his extensive writings on Aristotle were translated into Latin and Hebrew and available to readers of the day.

Ultimately, the church and scholars embraced Averroes and Aristotle. They trimmed away the element of mysticism in orthodox or mainstream Christianity, and a similar separation would occur in orthodox Islam. The Angel-Souls' intermediate realm ended up on the cutting room floor, as did the notion that humans could directly access the fullness of the divine with no intermediary. Ibn 'Arabi headed east and his mystical approach flowered there, albeit very quietly. He continued communicating with other-worldly beings and writing. The Angel-Souls didn't languish but belief in them faded, so sidelined in mainstream belief that not even the sound of children clapping could bring them back.

I feel gypped. I wish I'd had information about a possible intermediate realm and how to manage contact with it when at 10 years old beings from some other-worldly realm found their way into mine. Imagine living in a culture which is practiced in knowing the unknowable, talking about it, and the day comes when you get your first visit from a being from another realm. You may have already been initiated into this practice, or perhaps you will be initiated at the same time of your first visit. You are ready to apprehend the beings' nature and their message. Would your parents in this scenario pretend nothing had happened, and when pressed, say you had "a bad dream?" I'll bet not.

No one asked about my "bad dream." I didn't talk about it. I knew what I was encountering didn't exist. I didn't want to pursue that line of logic because I intuited where it could end.

Perhaps such illogical, intellectual resistance requires beings from those other realms to ante up on the props. "Wardrobe!" they shout; "Makeup!" For me, they donned cartoonish suits made of red and black metal and, in a fit of drama, communicated only telepathically. Others wore monkish hoods to hide their faces and tucked their hands in the pockets of plaid aprons. One woke me from sleep dressed in a smart black suit and a bowler hat, carrying a briefcase and gazing at me with phosphorescent green eyes; another appeared as a bronze giant on the side of Virginia State Highway 58 and another as a giant but gentle reptile in a swamp in South Carolina. Though the red and black metal beings just sat across from me at a table and supposedly communicated telepathically to me, I don't recall anything zinged into my brain. Only once did one friendly little beige give me a clear directive: "Get to know the lizard men of revelations; we need more of their kind." Right. Got it. I'm on it.

Our intermediate realm friends were equally showy when they made their bid for Major Nelson's attention. Even so, Jeannie had to help make the message clear: as the one who uncorked Jeannie's bottle, Major Nelson could wish for anything and Jeannie must grant it. But he was a man with a full life: a demanding job, good friends. An in-home genie was a nice-to-have. What would such a man wish for? Perhaps he wished for indifference and, in that way, tame his more animal instincts that must have prowled the perimeter with a buxom blonde in the house. He could have taken advantage of Jeannie's entrapment and had his way with her. Instead, he took his time getting to know her, establishing the rules, and, when the time was right, marrying her. Gentlemen wait and make the rules, even when the object of their love is a woman of power with supernatural connections.

The Goddess of Sloth

IT WAS FRIDAY MORNING AT the offices of Minnesota's largest higher education system. I worked at the machine in my cube. The beige walls rose high enough to block visuals but not aurals of the sea of cubes surrounding me. I could hear my coworkers filtering in, plunking down laptop bags, sighing, then tromping off to the kitchen to get coffee. Most of my coworkers had been out earlier in the week, attending our organization's annual IT conference a few hours north of our downtown St. Paul office. Friday was a good day to return to work. Only one day to go before the weekend.

I stood up in my cube to stretch, turning away from the beige metal shelves and twisting in a side stretch toward the main aisle. Down it strode tall Sam, our identity management specialist.

I meowed at him instead of saying hello.

Sam laughed and stopped at my cube. "That's just what

my cat did yesterday when I got home from the conference," he said.

When he'd arrived home the night before, the family cat had pounced on him, meowing frantically. She was "his cat;" her human was home. He cuddled her but to no avail; she meowed and meowed, so clearly hugs were not what she wanted. Carrying her, he went down the steps to the lower level to check her food bowl; it sat empty in its place at the bottom of the steps. She jumped from his arms the moment he reached for the cat food bag, and when he poured food into her bowl, she plowed face-first into the mound of food. Back upstairs, Sam asked his wife, teenage son and four-year-old daughter if any of them had fed the cat while he was away; sheepishly, they all said no. These were not acts of cruelty; his wife and children were just accustomed to Sam feeding the cat, and without an official request to take care of this while he was away, no one had thought to do it. Sam also didn't think to instruct anyone. He knew his four-year-old daughter often scooped out dry food for the cat on her way into the lower level. For some reason she didn't do this while he was away. Sam noted to me the cat was never in danger; she knew how to knock over the cat food bag, or at least knew how to do this when their other cat was alive. But he also noted she had probably been uncomfortable, hungry, and it bothered him knowing she'd experienced that level of distress.

When I told this story to Cierra, the graphic designer I work with who has also become my friend, she interpreted my instinctive meowing to mean I shifted into a cat persona and was thanking Sam on behalf of the feline species.

If so, I'm not sure what I was thanking him for. After all, he and his other familial humans had neglected to feed my soul sister, the family cat.

Once upon a time, I would have had the words at the ready in the forefront of my brain and the back of my throat to respond to Cierra. Instead, I thought but didn't say, "No, I just felt compelled to meow when I saw him." When it comes to intuition, what I intuit is so solid and clear to me that anyone offering a different interpretation doesn't even compute. Others' words do not prick me as they once did. As a result, the words that form in habitual response often rise up and fall back, unspoken.

I'm getting lazy. My role in the world in my younger years was somewhere between Athena and Artemis, Greek goddesses representing the roles of strategist and woman-unto-herself, respectively. My role in my internal world was represented by the Greek goddess Persephone, fated to spend half my life in the underworld.

Now I have become a lazy experiencer of the anomalous including strange intuitive encounters such as the one with Sam. I am more akin to Aergia, the Greek goddess of indolence and sloth. Once I let in whatever intelligence powered the more frightening paranormal encounters of my youth and middle age, I no longer had to assign an inner point-man to pace the psychic battlements for incoming. In classic Jungian fashion, once I let it in what was out there that external, extreme "other" became internalized, incorporated into who I am. The intelligence behind the beings in the encounters melted into mine; it no longer had to take on forms of fantastical beings outside of my consciousness. This meant more restful nights for me, and a new circuit of intelligence coursing through my brain. I no longer have to entertain beings from the spirit-world during three a.m. visits. I've heard it said visits from anomalous beings often occur in the early morning hours because we are most receptive at this time. Only the noise of our dreams is going on in our heads. With our bodies held captive by sleep, we are sufficiently passive.

More active methods of processing encounters with anomalous beings exist. Once I am done basking in the relaxing glow of uninterrupted nights of sleep, maybe I will investigate these.

Midwestern Medium

IN 2014, I MET BECKA, then 54, who lives in a rural area in the upper Midwest. The nearest city is three hours south, the Canadian border three hours north. Becka has lived in this area all her life, first with the family she was born into and, in her adult life, the family she married into.

"I started seeing stuff when I was four years old," said Becka. "That's my first recollection."

Becka hasn't encountered extraterrestrials in the forms prevalent in America media—"grays," "Nordics"—but has encountered dead or near-dead relatives as they exit this world and transition to the next. When Becka's kin are passing, she often experiences a physical sensation such as a light touch or a drop in temperature. This wakes her from sleep to witness her relatives' physical form as they make the transition or to receive messages from them in the form of their words entering her mind.

In October 2010, when Becka's mom lay ill in a cancer

care center near Becka's rural home, Becka was asleep in the bed she shares with her husband. A couple of hours past midnight the temperature in the room dropped, and Becka woke. The first thing that came to her mind was, "Mom. The Care Center." The room was so cold she could see her breath. She knew, she says, that her mom had passed. In fact, she had, at 1:50 a.m. that morning, at just about the same time the cold woke her from a deep sleep. Becka interprets the drop in temperature to mean her mom was trying to wake her as she passed. Her mother, Becka notes, also saw things, though Becka doesn't elaborate. On an earlier visit to her mom in the cancer care center, Becka said to her mom, "Just come and visit me in my dreams," to which her mom said, "I will." Like an elemental, her departing mother summoned the forces of climate to wake her daughter.

Becka's husband's grandfather had greater substance when he passed. He seemed to have access to his more corporeal affects and operated within the same laws of physics we are accustomed to in our waking lives. Becka lay asleep next to her husband, a similar setting as when her mother passed. This time, though, she'd been sick with strep throat. She was awakened by a touch to her foot. Her husband's grandfather, Grandpa B., stood at her bed, wearing the same clothes he typically wore before he'd fallen ill and went into the hospital—jeans and a flannel shirt. "I just stopped in to say goodbye," he said. Becka's impression was that he had already died and that his spirit was leaving. He wanted her to pass on the message of his passing. And so she did. She woke her husband and said, "Grandpa B. was just here." Two hours later, the nurse called to tell them he had passed. His time of death was within 15 minutes of when she saw him at the foot of her bed.

Becka told her mother-in-law, daughter of Grandpa B., what she had experienced, and her mother-in-law told her she also got a touch when she was asleep that night, only on her hand, not her foot, and with no accompanying vision of her father's physical form. However, she knew it was her father. She told Becka not to tell anyone because, as she put it, "They'd think I'm nuts."

Becka's husband's grandfather on the other side of his family—his father's father—also visited her as he passed. He woke her at 5:30 a.m. the morning of his passing. There was no touch; something just woke her up. Grandpa G. stood at the end of the bed. "Grandpa," Becka said. He smiled and faded away. She understood he'd stopped in to say goodbye.

After Grandpa G. faded away from where he stood at the foot of the bed, she woke her husband and told him his grandfather had died.

"These were super peaceful experiences," Becka notes. "When they occurred, it was as though the world had stopped." Even if she had tried, Becka says, nothing could stop what she was experiencing.

She has said to her husband, "I don't know why your relatives are coming to me. I'm just passing it on."

"To this day," Becka says, "I still don't know why."

She's not sure if she's more open. She doesn't will these experiences. They just happen. It's only family members who visit her.

Becka's father appeared to her three days after he died in 1975 when she was 15 years old. Death had dismembered him; only his head appeared, lifted toward the ceiling and surrounded by a glow. She heard his voice but his mouth wasn't moving. She felt he had come back to give a message and put her heart at ease. Becka says, "He had told me and Mom, 'Don't sell the farm.' It would be the salvation place for the whole family. The family needed to pull together." He spoke the same message to her mother.

To Becka, he ended by saying, "Goodbye for now." Becka says he didn't say it exactly like that but she knew that was what he meant.

Both she and her mom got the feeling he was watching over her.

She once said to her younger sister, "The spirit world is here with us." This particular sister has experienced what she described as the evil presence of spirits. She stopped believing, and then her experiences stopped.

Becka has never had bad experiences.

"I feel I may be a medium," Becka says. "There's times I've turned my back on it," said Becka, referring to her abilities.

Becka once asked her younger sister, "Why do you think I've gotten this gift?" Her sister replied, "Well, it can't be from God."

When Becka's brother learned she was speaking to me about her experiences, he showed her a recent digital photo he'd taken of her on her porch. A plume of white wavered behind Becka and had the rough form and facial features of a person. Becka, trusting, passed it on to me. We'd completed our interview by then. Shortly after, she wrote with me, deeply embarrassed, that her brother had faked the photo; he thought it a great joke to play on her.

Bad Mind

She apologized for wasting my time, and that was the last I heard from Becka.

Layers

I HAD SERVED AS THE goddess' bitch since I was 10 years old. Like the fictional Renfield in Bram Stoker's novel *Dracula* I was under another's power. The Throne who wielded that power visited me in the form of other-worldly beings. Had I been born into a different family or century perhaps I would have been sent off to the village shaman for training. As it was, I stumbled about on my own, finding solace and guidance in literature — poetry, fiction and Jungian writings, in particular Sylvia Brinton Perera's book *Descent to the Goddess: A Way of Initiation for Women*. Perera offers the Sumerian myth of Inanna as a metaphor for women's re-introduction to the feminine which has been banished for 5,000 years. The return of the feminine is fraught with peril, requiring dismemberment of previous identities.

The presence of other-worldly beings in my life rose to a shattering peak in August 1987 in Chuckatuck, Virginia.

After that time, I functioned as a change agent. If I entered someone's life, change was about to occur. If I started a new IT job, the corporate ranks were about to get shuffled. At times I felt like a leavening agent, like yeast added to warm water when baking bread. When I functioned that way in individuals' lives, change manifested; once it had, they moved on, all except my husband Tom who remains at my side.

By the time Hope entered my life, I was in the process of trying to surrender to what seemed to be my fate. I'd gone public; I'd published a memoir of my 30 years of encounters with anomalous beings and was speaking and teaching on the topic.

Hope Scoles attended the writing class I offered at The Metamorphosis Center on September 24, 2014, in Burnsville, a suburb of Minneapolis, Minnesota. Hope arrived at the center a few minutes late, apologizing to the center director who greeted attendees in the reception area. Hope entered our small meeting room smiling. The other students were just getting settled on the couches and in the chairs surrounding the long table in the softly lit room. I sat at one end of the table, the materials for the class in front of me. I told Hope not to worry; she was just in time.

Hope introduced herself. She was a psychologist and, at that time, a Higher Brain Living® Advanced Facilitator and Director for the Center of Alternative Healing[1]. She added, "My guides told me I had to show up for this class."

---

[1] *As of August 26, 2019, Hope's position has changed: she is Director for The Soul Growth Institute where she teaches psychology and spiritual growth classes.*

Bad Mind

I was accustomed to people speaking of their guides though I had never had the pleasure of invisible beings providing such clear direction. I'd had plenty of visitors of the extreme other variety — extraterrestrials, men in black, angels and demons, to name a few — so I wasn't in any position to question anyone who said they had such direction.

I began class, and the participants asked for my story, and so I shared the twin themes in my life that seem intertwined with my encounters with anomalous beings: always be perfect, always be working.

I auditioned for first grade when I was five years old. We were living in Brunswick, Georgia, where my dad was stationed at a nearby naval base. There was a kindergarten near our house but it was private. There was a nearby grade school, where my older sister went, but it had no kindergarten. My parents wanted me to be able to walk to school with my older sister. The grade school took me on a trial basis. As the principal stood with the teacher at the back of the first-grade classroom, watching me, I self-consciously walked past the crafts cabinets. The pocket of my plaid dress caught on one of the door handles as I passed by, jerking me back with the sound of ripping threads. I froze; I had not perfected the walk past the craft cabinets. Would the principal see this as failure and give me the boot? He didn't. Whatever his criteria were that day, I fit, and I got to stay and finish first grade, never having to step foot in kindergarten. However, the feeling of needing to be perfect or else suffer rejection never left me.

Five years later, when I was 10, my uninvited, other-worldly visitors began introducing me to their world. I felt compelled to go to work. In exchange for free lunch, I worked in the grade school cafeteria, standing next to one-eyed Mrs. Rus in our matching hairnets and white aprons. When we were done serving, Mrs. Rus stationed me next to a metal trashcan at the cafeteria's exit, spatula in my hand to scrape uneaten food from my classmates' trays.

Always be perfect, always be working. These were the twin themes that threaded through my life. They formed my life engine, the power source that guided my actions and choices. At different points in my life I'd sought therapists' help in understanding this, and they'd offered the more traditional, earth-bound explanations: the perfectionism my response to various factors present in the family in which I grew up, the relentless need to always be working essentially the same ("strong work ethic").

I paused in my short autobiographical introduction. I was planning to segue to the writing exercises, and in preparation began sorting through the papers in front of me to find the student handouts.

"Pristine calibration," Hope said from where she sat on the couch.

I stopped shuffling papers and looked up. I'd heard her but had no idea what she meant. "Say again?"

"I've known and worked with a few people who are gateways or portals," she said, "and that work requires precision when moving one being from one dimension into another. It requires 'pristine calibration.'" She smiled.

As I sat there, staring at Hope, I felt mental constructs shatter and fall away. My application of the mantra

"Always be perfect, always be working" to how I moved in the outer world melted away. The mantra's rightful heir slid into place: the constant work and constant perfection of functioning as a gateway for energies and perhaps even entities transforming from one state to another, one dimension to another.

Hope had carved new neural pathways in my brain with her words, and new streams of electric thought were buzzing along them. I just wanted to let them flow. Hope's face was radiant as she talked about experiencers who serve as gateways or portals. In her professional life she had encountered a few among the individuals who, after experiencing contact with other-worldly beings, sought her help. Those who seemed to function as gateways or portals often had layers between those roles and how they functioned in our waking world.

The layers seemed to function as disguised stand-ins for what the individuals were called to do in the spirit world. This was different from shadow, the term Jungians and other like-minded psychologists use for cast-off parts of a person's self. Shadow rejects the parts of yourself you find abominable and projects those qualities on other people. Layers served to bring other-worldly functions into this world, the one we call reality. The experiencer might struggle against the role in the outer world and feel fated to carry it out. Revealing the face of the function beneath its outer-world mask was the antidote.

Hope had swept us all up; the class members leaned forward in their seats as she spoke, their faces lit with curiosity and new ways of thinking. A part of me kept thinking I should try to return to the original focus of the class, the writing exercises I had developed to integrate the effects of encounters with anomalous beings, but I could feel that was pushing against the tide.

As someone who had adopted the masculine approach to the world — i.e., might is right — I knew how to use it, even though in recent years it had stopped serving me as well. Even so, in situations like this, where I was the leader and had a job to do, I felt the need to override the unanticipated flow of the class with the stated agenda. People had paid to take the class; they would be expecting to get what they paid for, even if it did take place at a venue with the word "metamorphosis" in its name.

The center director and owner was in the class, and when the conversation paused, I asked everyone how they would like to proceed: would they like to continue the discussion or find our way back to the writing exercises? Unanimously, the class members voted to continue the discussion, and the center director nodded her approval. I let go of trying to steer the discussion back to its original topic.

For a few moments, I stopped working in our outer world. I may not have entirely removed that layer of "always be working," but for a little while I pulled it back. How I moved in the outer world didn't need to reflect my real "job": serving as a gateway or portal, allowing other beings to move from one dimension to another and other humans to move from one stage to another.

Layers may represent resistance; they may also represent a cushion wisely provided by that intelligence behind other-worldly encounters. That intelligence may be known as the goddess, the divine feminine, beings from the spirit-world, extraterrestrials, extradimensionals, angels and many other names. Their manifestations in our waking world may be like twins in dreams: the qualities they represent are still not quite in focus. As experiencers work to bring these qualities into focus, understanding and integrating the effects of encounters with extreme other, they may place the central energy of the encounters outside themselves and see it as a force working on them.

This is similar to a rhythm Nichola Torbett, founding director of Seminary of the Street, has described about Americans' relationship with their inner lives. Americans respond to a pull or need to tend to their inner worlds by doing the reverse: they go out. They take classes in working with their inner selves, join book clubs to read about spirituality and sign up for meditation sessions, all in order to prepare themselves to, at some theoretical point, heed the call to turn inward. As Nichola put it, we go out to go in.

Americans seem to have this same rhythm in their relationship with largely invisible worlds. We pursue ideas and approaches in the outer world with the intent of using them, maybe someday, to aid the inner work required to connect with beings of an extreme other nature.

The class I taught at The Metamorphosis Center in September 2014 was exactly that. I invited people to come out to go in. Thanks to her guides, Hope came by and shattered the original approach, Kali-like, with her lightning bolt of words.

Since that September night, the veil between me and the anomalous beings who visited me for so many years began to thin. Less and less did they need dreams or the cover of darkness to visit me.

One night I woke to find what appeared to be a demon the size of a cat curled up and sleeping on my chest. It opened its eyes and, with a look of surprise, registered me looking at it. Then it dissolved. When I told Hope about this, her take was that I had glimpsed a being as it moved along its transformational journey for which I served as a gateway.

Then, in the early evening of March 12, 2015, as I sat at the dining room table, I heard a clear voice say, "We're coming." It felt telepathic more than auditory.

That night I woke up inside a dream to tell my husband of this dream: a presence had filled our bedroom, manifesting as mist and a low hum, like a long, drawn out "oh." It was there to do work on my soul, which it completed and then left.

The morning after that dream-inside-a-dream, I luxuriated in the bath as I got ready for my IT day job. The warm water felt good. I was — and am — hobbled by wear-and-tear physical conditions, osteoarthritis and spinal stenosis caused by degenerating joints and discs. As I lay in the warm water, I began to feel a sense of separation between what I do at a soul level and what my life looks like in the waking world. They need not be aligned.

I was able to hold on to this lovely concept for a few days. When I rejoined my fellow humans in our waking-world endeavors, what little progress I had made took several steps back. Then I was back to viewing reality from my earthly body. As long as I was in this terrestrial form, I couldn't make the jump to consistently holding advanced thinking. I couldn't willingly sever my sensual connection with my realm; I always returned to my physical body and my senses. This is true for a fictional counterpart, Al·lith in Doris Lessing's novel *The Marriages Between Zones Three, Four, and Five (as narrated by the Chroniclers of Zone Three)*. After loss propels Al·lith into her first mystical journal into the thin, blue air of Zone Two, where "her imaginings of its immaculate fire-born beings brought her near them," she wakes in the morning, alone, and consumed by her physical longings. She is a "vast hungry ache" for Yori her horse, which had died the day before, and for her husband, who was ordered to marry another queen, but one from "the barbarous and backward" Zone Five. She suppresses that ache, and, bedraggled, wanders into a village where she is mistaken for a beggar. At the suggestion of the woman who gives her stale bread she finds work caring for the horses and the cows and waits to learn her fate, "alertly, and on her guard.

The narrator of Lessing's novel, known only as a Chronicler, reveals, hesitantly, that disparate realms must interact with each other to continue life: "without this sting of otherness, of — even — the vicious, without the terrible energies of the underside of health, sanity, sense, then nothing works or *can* work." This "sting of otherness," which, the Chronicler notes, has a spectrum, can cause a person to examine their less palatable sides, not a pleasant prospect: "We Chroniclers do well to be afraid when we approach those parts of our histories (our natures) that deal with evil, the depraved, the benighted." Even more alarming, according to the Chronicler, our goodness—"what we in our ordinary daylight selves call goodness"—is "nothing without the hidden powers that pour forth continually from their shadow sides." The shadow feeds the light and vice versa: "The very high must be matched by the very low... even fed by it... but that is not a thought I can easily accommodate or that I wish to write much of." With you on that one, Chronicler.

I suspect I don't have Al·lith's mettle to entirely suppress what connects me to this world; however, I can follow the lead of the anonymous Chronicler who writes, "Describing, we become." As my outer-self sheds like my physical skin, slowly and leaving a trail of dust, I watch and describe. The less identity I have, the better, it seems, I function as a gateway, a portal through which energies pass.

For a time, I offered Reiki in the pre-dawn hours to anyone who requested it and was willing to share their birthdate and geographical location. I've sent it to an acquaintance with an achy back, to two affectionate but misbehaving hounds, and to a very ill friend on the North Shore of the island of Oahu. I've sent it to the nephew of a friend who, for a time, was hospitalized for mental illness. I could hear him speaking to me in a muffled voice each night as I offered the distance Reiki. Perhaps one day he will recount this experience as a visit from an uninvited, other-worldly visitor.

By understanding the reality of our invisible spirit world, not the unreal notions I once entertained about it, I may just have a chance to grow up and become better acquainted with the beings who populate that world. I don't think they are here to bring us love and light, much like the nameless movers in Lessing's novel who shift people from Zone to Zone so that life and renewal may continue.

A Visit to Usha's

A THIN, BURNISHED MAN IN a turban and loin cloth weaves in and out of the stopped automobiles, autorickshaws and motor bikes of Bangalore traffic. The man holds aloft paper towels. I need to remember to ask for Kleenex at the hotel. A cow ambles alongside the road. The traffic starts up again, and the driver of our open-sided autorickshaw wheels the miniature vehicle into the heavy traffic.

My co-workers Shyam and Devyani are squeezed with me into the back of the auto. Our knees are inches from the back of the driver's seat. Our driver sits in the middle of his bench and faces the broad, curved glass windshield. He wheels the auto into the heavy traffic. I breathe in the soupy exhaust and grip the iron handrail as we career around corners.

We are on our way to visit Usha. My stateside co-worker

Katy, a rock collector, has asked that I bring her a rock from Bangalore, and, by coincidence or luck, Shyam's cousin Usha happens to collect rocks.

"What do you think, Karen?" Shyam asks, shouting.

"About what?" I shout back, leaning into them.

Both Shyam and Devyani look at me and laugh then resume their shouted conversation they have tried but failed to include me in.

The driver slides the auto into the merging traffic. Three- and four-wheelers jam around us and honk. Our driver leaps out and pushes the auto backwards. Shyam and Devyani look at me and laugh.

"He's going the wrong way," Shyam explains. "He's getting us turned around."

Shyam jumps out of the Auto, followed by Devyani who says, "Come on, Karen."

On foot, we wind through the stopped, honking traffic. Shyam approaches a car. He opens the front door and motions me to get in the front with the woman driver. He and Devyani and get in back.

"Karen," says Shyam from the back seat, "meet my cousin Usha."

"Did you plan this?" I ask.

"No, no," says Usha, as the traffic starts back up and she weaves into it. "It's entirely coincidental. I was at work and Shyam called to let me know you were coming over. I left assuming I'd be late but knew my husband could greet you. And suddenly there you were next to me in traffic."

Usha veers off the main road into a long alley where she and the drivers of oncoming vehicles vie for the right-of-way. She honks and steers head-on into the other cars' headlights, a game of Bangalore chicken won by the driver with the steeliest nerves. Each time Usha remains the victor.

"There's no traffic signs, just traffic nonsense," Usha says as we fly through the alleys. The lights from the small, open-air stalls that line the road strobe.

As Usha pulls into her driveway, the car lights beam into a tree, transfixing a girl sitting in the branches. Startled, the girl falls out, landing cat-like on her feet, then twirls away into the darkness of the yard. Usha shakes her head.

We walk across the courtyard and enter a separate entrance to Usha's rock room. She keeps her stones and gems in two glass cases and on a bookshelf between them. The three of us, Devyani, Usha and I, bend over the cases and look at the rocks.

Usha picks up a rock and hands it to me. It's large, flat and green.

"What is this?" she asks.

I hold it and consider. "Something to do with water?"

She says, "It's all water. Come on, you know."

I look at Devyani, and she looks blankly back at me.

"Aquamarine," says Usha.

"This one," she says, holding up a large white rock with black ridges jutting out at the top.

I study its milky, sparkly finish. "Quartz?"

"Yes. And the black?"

I haven't a clue. Then a word forms somewhere on the back of my tongue and comes rolling out. "Tourmaline?"

"Yes," Usha says.

Usha brings out a small box of stones, and one catches my

eye. "Green tourmaline," she says.

"This one seems right for Katy," I say. I ask how much it is and pay for it in rupees.

As Usha places the green tourmaline in a small plastic bag she says, "It's rare to be able to purchase stones in Bangalore. You would not have been able to find someone selling them on your own. They are here and there but hidden."

The girl from the tree brings in our tea. She hands me my cup from a tray, dipping her face toward mine. The lids of her eyes aren't symmetrical—one lid rises in peaks near the lash line.

Usha, Devyani and I sit between the cases of rocks and drink our sweet, milky tea. Usha's face lights up when I mention I have been to see Arun H.S., an Iyengar yoga teacher in Bangalore.

"He is one of the greatest masters of yoga in India," she says. "Did you know that? When Mr. Iyengar comes to visit Bangalore, he stays with Arun."

Usha has traveled all over the world except the U.S. "Too hard," she says, and Devyani nods in agreement. "You have to camp out in front of the U.S. embassy in Delhi a day before your interview."

We rise to leave. We walk into the warm night air, and Shyam goes into the alley to find us an auto.

A four-wheeler or SUV pulls up, and it is Usha's husband. Two other men get out with him but only he enters the yard.

"He has his driver with him," Usha notes. She doesn't mention who the other fellow is.

Bad Mind

Her husband bustles into the courtyard where Usha's father-in-law has joined us under the tree our tea server fell from earlier.

Usha introduces Devyani and me to her husband and father-in-law. We all fold our hands to our chest and say, "Namaskar." I say it like an American, enunciating each of the three syllables. The others pronounce it as though it is made entirely of vowels; it slides out of their mouths like water.

We get in the autorickshaw Shyam has found for us. Our driver veers in and out of four-wheelers in the beeping, roaring traffic. Shyam directs us to get out of the auto about half a block before the restaurant which is off on the main road a side street. The three of us walk along the footpath.

"Watch out," Devyani says and takes my arm. We skirt a pothole of rubble and mud. "Another one," she says as she pulls me away from a mini crater.

We come into the light of the restaurant entryway. "Rice Bowl," the sign reads. Shyam motions for Devyani and I to sit on the bench, then disappears down the stairs into the restaurant. In a few minutes Shyam comes back for us and leads us down.

The stucco ceiling is low, and the lighting is dim. Another co-worker, Vijay, waves to us from our table in the corner.

I ask where the restroom is, and the waiter motions for me to follow him. We weave through the restaurant. All the walls have large, buttery-yellow squares painted in the middle, framed by mahogany-colored wood. I hope I can find my way back. Inside the bathroom my hopes rise when I spy toilet paper, soap and paper towel dispensers. Alas, they are gestures; all are empty.

Doused in Purell, I leave the bathroom and happily spot my coworkers so my trek back to the table is easy. There are the usual stares and head-turnings. In contrast to everyone else's dark hair and skin, I must glow as though I'm irradiated.

Devyani gives me another Ganesh, a deep red elephant-headed figure. Earlier in the day, at the office, she gave me one shaped like an iridescent dollop of whipped cream to put on my monitor back in the U.S. Faced outward to the door, Ganesh helps ensure success in work endeavors.

"You can never have too much Ganesh," I say, and she laughs.

After dinner we climb the steps back up to street level.

As Devyani goes with Shyam to find an auto, Vijay says to me, "Tonight was groundbreaking. We had dinner with a manager, something so easy and common in the U.S. This has never happened before here. India has rigid hierarchies, and we are breaking those, too."

The next morning at work I go into the pantry or break room for water. Mohit the office boy is busy, washing the teacups in the sink. Surely, just this once, it will be okay for me to get my own water. I reach out to open the refrigerator door. Others in the pantry gasp. Mohit drops his soapy cup in the sink, dashes to my side and grabs for the refrigerator door. Mohit and I fumble as we both try to retract our hands. Mohit opens the door, retrieves a bottle of water and hands it to me.

At the front desk of the hotel at the workday's end, I request Kleenex.

Bad Mind

The fellow looks at me blankly.

"Tissues," I say, and he nods.

A short while later, a knock sounds at my door. A smiling hotel staff member hands me a tiny packet of 10 tissues. For the first time here in India my heart sinks. I need more! At the same moment I realize just exactly how American I am.

Ten years pass. I no longer work for that technology company that sent me in 2005 to our office in Bangalore, India. I married at 47, which is old for a first-time American bride. Apparently, I can't both be married and work at a permanent, full-time job, as though I'm Clark Kent who can't be in the same room as Superman at the same time. I've lost several jobs through downsizing and bad luck or overweening optimism, when I took jobs well above my pay grade. The universe tested my mettle, and I failed. The failure resulted in a cleft opening in my sense of my self, a breach between who I imagined I could be in the world and who I actually was. I turned inward, descended, and shifted my focus to my own strange experiences with inexplicable things and energies. Monica Furlong writes of the "seismic inner vent" that opens up in a person and allows them or forces them to fall into the netherworld of the mystic and seer. Medieval woman mystic Julian of Norwich fell into this psychic chasm when she was on what she thought was her deathbed and received visions of the divine. Mine was less of a "seismic inner vent" and more of a cranny. I was no Julian of Norwich. However, I began to more deeply explore my other-worldly experiences, including that night with Usha when she pulled names of stones out of me like a shaman releasing trapped spirits.

I found my old co-worker Shyam on linkedin.com. He passed on to me Usha's telephone number and email address. I emailed Usha. I told her about the areas of experience I was exploring and asked her about that night.

She wrote me as bursting crackers, or firecrackers, exploded outside her home. She was celebrating Diwali, the festival of lights.

"They are deafening," she wrote.

That very month, Usha went on in her email, she and her husband welcomed their little granddaughter into the world, and Usha completed her astrology second-year midterm exam.

As our email communication progressed, we discovered that our paths and thinking were converging on certain points: How can westerners and easterners blend their approaches to personal power and offer each other their strengths?

"Sometimes I feel maybe it's time to amalgamate both," Usha wrote. "For the modern psyche is a product of both east and west."

I recounted for Usha how as she showed me her rocks and gems she seemed to pull knowledge out of me that I didn't know I had. The rocks she showed me were not rocks I'd encountered before, and I truly didn't know their names. However, when she presented each rock to me and asked me its name, somehow she pulled the names out of me; they came tumbling out of my mouth, my tongue and lips forming words as though learning them that instant.

In response, Usha wrote,

> It's true that many people experience an altered state of consciousness during a session. Very often during a session people are able to tap into memory which lies in the deeper layers of the mind, most often these are pockets which the conscious mind prefers to not acknowledge. These hidden aspects emerge during a reading because of the energy of the cards + the energy of the healing stones. Incidentally, India is a home to many types of healing stones.

While I thought I went to find a stone for Katy, had I actually signed on for a healing session? Perhaps I melted into Usha's world, where she exists as a subtle source of power, a conduit between the divine and earthly life. I tend to melt into situations, like heated wax into the weave of a piece of cloth. This quality is so much a part of my nature I am often not conscious of it.

I mentioned to Usha that I felt refreshed that night after our visit.

"The effect of a reading session is varied," she wrote. "Most often people are left feeling inspired."

During my time with beings of power, I can say this about the different types and their affects: an eastern woman of power such as Usha, born and bred in modern India with its history of colonization and political changes, I left feeling my energy had been restored. After encounters with Americans of power, whether writers, yogis or business people, I felt jangled, aroused and expectant—seduced.

"You are right about Americans sending out their power in the form of seduction," Usha wrote, and suggested I

watch a Hindi movie *English-Vinglish.*
She continued,

> My observation has been that westerners find it very easy to express themselves; maybe at times they appear to be a little flamboyant. However, in India especially in the times when we were growing up we were always taught to respect our elders by merely accepting their decisions without rebellion. For they always worked for our good. This almost stole our voice. The best thing would be to strike a balance. Which many of us are working at. The current generation is certainly different.

Though Usha is an entrepreneur, the owner of a women's clothing business, she offers all she does to the divine. She is a woman of power in the business and esoteric worlds but functions more as a conduit than a sole energy source manifesting in the material world. I asked her how her personal power affects or feeds into the business she owns and runs.

"My work is totally taken care of by the divine," she responds. "I do not advertise, do not have a website, no visiting cards. Yet my days are loaded with work. I travel extensively, work in studios abroad and I totally avoid being covered by the press."

Usha attributes this approach to her Indian culture and upbringing. "India is an ancient culture going back many centuries," she wrote. "Remember, India was getting into slavery while Americans were hoisting their flag of independence. We are taught to offer all that we do to the divine. Whether it is dance, music, hair, food... This is established through rituals, which begin from the time we are in our mother's womb to the time we reach our tomb."

What does an American such as myself do in the absence of rituals? I have my American rituals — my coffee in a throw-away cup, online shopping and compulsions I enact like a child touching her stuffed animals in a certain order each night before sleep.

Usha was kind in her acknowledgement that both east and west have their strengths.

"Each has something very precious for the other," she wrote in her January email of both approaches.

That November Usha was balancing her life between two worlds. Her new little granddaughter was "struggling to establish herself on this earth" and her mother was "struggling to cut the chords that hold her to the earth."

Life and death pulled Usha away. We haven't corresponded since. Our lives touched twice, and I'm content with that and not wishing for more. Maybe someday I can apply that to my love of paper products. No wonder the aliens rarely show me their faces; the ones who have connected with me and my kin probably got the short end of the straw when pulling for jobs around the galaxy. "Oh no," I can imagine them murmuring, "not another human."

Earlier when I wrote Usha of my impressions of Indian personal power versus American, in response she noted Indians are more comfortable with spirit, and westerners, particularly Americans, are more comfortable with manifestation:

We human being have two currents flowing through us — a current descending from above called the manifesting current and another current from earth which moves upward called the liberating current. As I have seen for us Indians, we have a strong liberating current, hence it is easy for us to understand the matters of the spirit. Whereas, for westerners the current of manifestation is strong and hence are very good with their manifesting abilities.

Perhaps Usha has hit on why the aliens rarely show us their true faces but find themselves inexplicably attracted to our kind.

Endnotes

http://www.vocabulary.com/dictionary/quantum%20leap

Gerry Goddard: "Uranus, Neptune, Pluto (Our Contemporary Evolutionary Challenge)," revised version: March 2003. http://cura.free.fr/xxv/25god2.html.

In November 2012 the United States Department of Justice settled with BP Oil on federal charges of manslaughter, misdemeanors and a felony count of lying to Congress. In September 2014, a U.S. District Court judge ruled that BP was "primarily responsible for the oil spill because of its gross negligence and reckless conduct." In July 2015, BP agreed to pay $18.7 billion dollars in fines, "the largest corporate settlement in U.S. history. https://en.wikipedia.org/wiki/Deepwater_Horizon_oil_spill

A 2013 study showed dolphins and other marine life continued to die in record numbers, with high rates of mortality among the infant dolphins. A 2014 study showed tuna and amberjack had developed deformities of the heart and other organs. https://en.wikipedia.org/wiki/Deepwater_Horizon_oil_spill

Due to space restrictions, only some of the details of Chris' encounters are shared here. With Chris' permission I have recorded all of his experiences to date in a longer document. Chris has also granted me permission to publicly share his experiences and to use his first name.

Interviews, June 2015. Unless otherwise noted all other quotes and references to Chris' experiences are from the two phone interviews that took place on June 6 and June 13 in 2015.

https://en.wikipedia.org/wiki/Deepwater_Horizon_oil_spill

Ibid.

Ibid.

Chris has an ancient corollary in this: St. Anthony was an early Christian solitary who lived in towns and cities around Upper Egypt in about 300 CE. Like Chris, St. Anthony gave his mind, body and spirit to what called him, which, in St. Anthony's case, was solitude in an abandoned Roman fort and battling demons, according to James Reho in "When God is a Sheep in a Wolf's Clothing," an article which appears in the Summer 2015 issue of *Parabola*. St. Anthony shared beliefs with Christian thinkers of the first century CE who saw our personhood rooted in its dual nature of body and spirit. This meant bringing all who you were into whatever was confronting you. For St. Anthony doing this appeared to grant the demons a physicality in this world. When visitors to St. Anthony's solitary retreat chatted with him at the fort's gate, they could hear the demons' voices inside the walls of the fort.

After reading of my experience in which dream images of white feathers involved in extraterrestrials metamorphosing into our dimension manifested as physical white feathers littering the floor of my house, Chris woke to find a white feather in his room on the boat. "My pillows aren't made of feathers," he notes. Personal communication, January 7, 2015.

Granite Publishing, 1991.

Bio, s.v. Nicholas Copernicus, accessed December 14, 2015, http://www.biography.com/people/nicolaus-copernicus-9256984

Mark Brake, *Alien Life Imagined: Communicating the Science and Culture of Astrobiology* (Cambridge: Cambridge University Press, 2013), 63.

Ingrid D. Rowland, *Giordano Bruno: Philosopher / Heretic* (New York: Farrar, Straus and Giroux, 2008), 277.

Jen Gerson, "Q&A: Retired McGill University professor convinced 'beyond a reasonable doubt' that aliens exist," *National Post*, February 25, 2013, http://news.nationalpost.com/news/canada/qa-retired-mcgill-university-professor-convinced-beyond-a-reasonable-doubt-that-aliens-exist

Don Donderi, Ph.D., *UFOs, ETs, and Alien Abductions* (Charlottesville, Virginia: Hampton Roads Publishing Company, Inc. 2013).

John E. Mack, *Abduction: Human Encounters with Aliens* (New York: Maxwell Macmillan International, 1994).

Philip J. Klass, "Mack's Harvard Tenure Reportedly Threatened By Faculty Investigation," *The Skeptics UFO Newsletter*, March 1, 1995, http://www.csicop.org/specialarticles/show/klass_files_volume_32/, paragraph 32.

"John E. Mack," *Contemporary Authors Online* (Detroit: Gale, 2007), *Biography in Context*, Web. 23 Dec. 2015.

Peter Sturrock et al., "Physical evidence Related to UFO Reports," proceedings of a workshop held at the Pocantico

Conference Center, Tarrytown, NY, September 29 – October 4, 1997 (Published in *Journal of Scientific Exploration*, vol. 12, no. 2, 179-229, quoted in John E. Mack, *Passport to the Cosmos: Human Transformation and Alien Encounters* (New York: Crown Publishers, 1999), 22. Mack references pages 183 and 184 of the report.

Ibid., 181.

"Mortificatio," narrated by Llorraine Neithardt, Venus Unplugged, December 14, 2015, www.blogtalkradio.com, about 14:10.

C.G. Jung, *The Red Book: Liber Novus,* Philemon Series, edited by Sonu Shamdasani (New York: W. W. Norton & Company, 2009), 200.

The names in this incident have been changed.

https://philosophynow.org/issues/33/Mary_Daly

Matthew is a fictitious name for a real person. I use a fictitious name to protect his privacy. He granted me permission to use his stories when I met him in Antigua in January 2015.

Boston: Shambhala, 1988, vii.

New York: Anchor Books, 1994, 112.

Linda is the real first name of a real person. She granted me permission to refer to her to her this way and to use her story.

San Diego, CA: Harvest/Harcourt Brace, 1976, 62.

Amity wishes to keep her identity private so I'm not using her real name in the essay.

Mack, John E. *Passport to the Cosmos.* New York: Crown Publishers, 1999, 34. "For an individual [a worldview] holds the psyche together. To destroy someone's worldview is virtually to destroy that person."

Recounted in detail in a separate essay, "Fairies on Big Island."

Becka is a pseudonym I'm using to protect her privacy, even though originally she granted me permission to use her real first name.

Sylvia Brinton Perera, *Descent to the Goddess* (Toronto: Inner City Books), 1981.

Hope granted me permission to use her real first and last name and note her profession and where she currently works.

Seminary of the Street is a nonprofit institute for the spiritual formation of social change workers in the context of community. Nichola shared her views with me in personal conversations in approximately 2003.

New York: Vintage Books, 1981.

Ibid., 199.

Ibid., 199 and 200.

Ibid., 200.

Ibid., 198.

Ibid., both 198.

Ibid., 198.

Ibid., 198.

Ibid., 198.

Usha granted me permission to quote her in a personal communication dated October 30, 2015, and permission to use her first name in a personal communication dated August 29, 2019.

Visions and Longings: Medieval Women Mystics (Boston, MA: Shambhala), April 15, 1997, 33.

Personal communication, November 11, 2015.

Personal communication, January 6, 2016.

Ibid. Usha further noted, "Modern psychology acknowledges the effect of rituals on the psyche. An important book here is one written by Murray Hope. The psychology of ritual."

Personal communication, November 27, 2015.

Ibid. In this email Usha noted, "I have been fortunate to read very good works of westerners. Here are some good writers whose works have inspired me: Anodea Judith, Erin Sullivan and & Liz Greene."

About the Author

Karen Cavalli, née Lound, writes fiction and non-fiction. Her work has been published online and in books and has won awards including Outstanding Secondary Science Book. She is a graduate of Old Dominion University where she earned a B.A., and The University of Alabama's MFA in Creative Writing Program where she studied with Margaret Atwood. She has worked in technology for over 10 years. She taught a writing course on the topic of psychological descent at the University of Minnesota and in North Carolina. Her work in technology has taken her to India and China and allowed her to work with individuals in Mexico, the United Kingdom, Australia, New Zealand and the emirate of Dubai. She loves her local Savage library and volunteers there. She is married to Tom Cavalli. She can be contacted at kcgoodguide@gmail.com

www.ingramcontent.com/pod-product-compliance
Lightning Source LLC
Chambersburg PA
CBHW052158110526
44591CB00012B/1993